PHILIP BARFORD

BRUCKNER
Symphonies

BBC MUSIC GUIDES

ARIEL MUSIC
BBC PUBLICATIONS

Published by BBC Publications
A division of BBC Enterprises Ltd
35 Marylebone High Street, London W1M 4AA

ISBN 0 563 20512 1

First published 1978
First published in Ariel Music, with revisions, 1986

Printed in England by Mackays of Chatham Ltd, Kent

Contents

N.B.—Bar numberings refer to the miniature study scores of the International Bruckner Society, ed. Leopold Nowak.

For Gwynneth, Jonathan and Adrian,
in memory of a journey we have made together

Anton Bruckner and his Symphonies

Anton Bruckner's birthplace was the quiet village of Ansfelden, just south of Linz. The house in which he was born in 1824, at the end of the short Augustinerstrasse, is austerely peaceful, and stands in the ambience of the church rising immediately behind it. A stepped passageway at the side of the house leads straight to the church porch.

The road to St Florian rises out of the village and leads over gentle, wooded hills characteristic of this part of Upper Austria. On the way it diminishes to a narrow, unpaved track through a magical forest which stimulates a wealth of romantic associations expressed in many Austrian and Bavarian folk-songs. Bruckner must have known it well. The peace and beauty of the region, and its haunting atmosphere, explain much about Austrian romanticism and about Bruckner's music. On a summer afternoon one's mood is exactly conveyed by the almost inaudible vibration with which the composer opens his Fourth Symphony; it would not seem surprising if its romantic horn-call sounded softly through the trees.

At St Florian, the great religious foundation is a natural focus of interest. The composer's body now lies in the vault under the huge organ, attended by thousands of skulls. The beautiful little Marian shrine which stands near a house associated with him in the busy main street of the town is more reassuring, and may serve as a reminder that Bruckner also composed profoundly inspired music for the church as well as symphonies and a fine quintet.

In fact, surface impressions may seem to confirm the image of Anton Bruckner as 'God's musician'. In him the religious life of romantic Austria found musical expression. Was the composer not born in the very shadow of the church? The music-lover steeped in the symphonies of Bruckner, responsive to the ethos of scholarship and contemplation which broods over St Florian, may feel that the traditional image is entirely appropriate; yet there is another very human aspect.

Bruckner was a short, nervous man with country ways, who shambled about Vienna in a baggy suit. His physical appearance, extremely typical of Upper Austria (there are men living there today who look like his blood-brothers), proclaimed his rural origins. His Prussian haircut contradicted the romantic image cultivated by late nineteenth-century composers. He was unsuccessful with women, and irritating to influential people, especially to Franz Liszt, who tended to keep out of his way. Bruckner was neither socially nor physically equipped for the inner circles of a sophisticated society. He was defenceless against the savage cut and thrust of Hanslick's criticism, and unable to prevent even his friends from mutilating his work when, having misunderstood it, they believed they could improve it. It is easy to see how he must have felt himself barred from areas of human discourse to which others less gifted and less industrious than he gained easy access. Inhibited by religious-moral restraint and his natural hesitancy and anxiety, he turned his creative energies towards music, countering his sense of inadequacy by arming himself with as many academic qualifications as possible.

He had a strange interest in tragedy and the macabre, no doubt born of an abiding sense of the omnipresence of death. In Central Europe the bones heaped up in church vaults can strike a melancholy note, especially when glimpsed from outside through an iron grille. One can wander through Austria with a mind increasingly sensitive to the limitations of human life and the immensities beyond it. The wayside shrines and crucifixes are as common as the ossuaries, silent companions of those who labour in the fields. It is possible that in Bruckner's imagination the dividing line between sombre awareness of the common lot and a morbid interest in death was not always clear. In the Ninth Symphony, the path to the concluding serenity of the *Adagio* crosses many a long shadow before sinking into a dreamlike peace. Yet his music is free of that kind of neurotic introspection characteristic of Mahler's; and it is the very opposite of death-centred.

The openings of Bruckner's symphonies are often born in a shimmering mystery reminiscent of the first sounds heard in Beethoven's Ninth; they are the first stirrings of a vast, cathedral-like space of harmony within which a huge tonal structure is going to take form. The symphonies have no programme and they call for objectivity in analysis. Nevertheless, Symphonies '0', 1, 2, 3, 7, 8 and 9 all contain themes from the four great Masses and Requiem composed between 1848 and 1868, and it is obvious that the *Benedictus* from the F minor Mass bears significantly upon Bruckner's conception of what a symphonic slow movement should sound like. The ethos of the mass and the registration of the St

Florian organ pervade certain aspects of his style.[1] Add to this the very attractive medium, aglow with Wagnerian brass and meditative woodwind, shot through with evocative horns and carried along with surges of string tone, and the symphonies offer an experience of creative integration not easily described.

Bruckner tends to work with monolithic blocks, each constructed around its own central idea. Frequently these are separated by pauses. Such moments of silence called forth harsh critical comment in Bruckner's day, especially in the case of the Second Symphony, which the composer himself nicknamed his *Pausensymphonie*; but they seem to be essential to his compositional technique, as if a statement has been made which must be pondered. They may also stem from unconscious reminiscence of organ improvisation. When improvising in a large, resonant church, there is a tendency to pause after *fortissimo* climaxes to give the vibrations time to settle down before beginning another section.

The enormous movements with which Bruckner begins and ends his symphonies do not synthesise their material in conventional ways. It is therefore misleading, especially when listening to the later works, to expect familiar sonata-form procedures. Bruckner's forms grow from adventurous harmonic relations arising from a late-romantic conception of harmony and chromatically-inflected melody. It frequently happens that these are prefigured in significant opening themes, as in the Sixth and Seventh Symphonies. Form, for Bruckner, is thus harmony writ large, and the dialectical tensions set up by conflicting tonal centres generate a huge, slowly-unfolding rhythmic organisation. Climaxes rise and wane, separated by pauses, chorale-like passages, or interludes of reflective counterpoint. The interludes are generally 'block-scored' for woodwind, brass or strings. On first acquaintance, Bruckner may sound wayward – until the ear accustoms itself to the inevitable, logical swing of his forms towards tonic major harmony; and then the effect is like the majestic orbital movement of the planet Saturn.

Superficially considered, such a technique seems Wagnerian. In listening to Wagner's music, Bruckner enjoyed the shifting

[1] See H. Redlich, *Bruckner and Mahler* (London, 1955), Ch. VIII, IX and X. The writer is also much indebted for information on this subject, and for a stimulating correspondence on Bruckner's religious background, to Michael Dawney, Lecturer in Music, University of Cork, who has undertaken special research in this field.

harmonies and their final resolutions intrinsically, and paid little attention to their dramatic implication. Nevertheless, Wagner's harmonic progressions were the tonal vehicle of drama, and it is now clear that music drama, for Wagner, had a symbolic, inward aspect. Of this Bruckner would have had little conscious awareness; but it is highly likely that the sounds he heard in Wagner were subconsciously reinterpreted in terms of another kind of interior drama which had the deepest significance for him – and that is the liturgical drama of the Mass. This may explain why the slow movements seem to glow with a contemplative, even prayerful depth of feeling, entirely free from self-indulgent emotionalism. The beautiful slow movement of the Seventh Symphony stirs mind and heart intensely before subsiding into nirvanic calm. To what extent his symphonies had inner symbolic meanings for the composer must remain conjectural. For the listener they offer a deeply satisfying musical experience culminating in a radiance rarely achieved by any other composer. The entire symphonic experience explored by Bruckner is integrative, spanning immensities as it searches for final tonic statement. In the way he ended his symphonies, Bruckner emerges as one of the last great composers (along with Mahler in the Eighth Symphony) whose use of the major triad touches deep springs of emotion and insight.

Bruckner initiates his symphonic arguments with momentous thematic statements. The final pages unfold a glory of sound which is only latent in the beginnings. The symphonies are not merely cyclical but 'elliptical'. The orbit of tonal movement swings round different harmonic polarities, and on the returning arc everything is changed. Perhaps the most striking example of this is the Eighth Symphony, which transfigures its opening theme in a tremendous contrapuntal fusion with the other main themes of the work in the culminating tonic major harmony.

Bruckner and Mahler are often paired in short historical surveys and informal critical discussion; but their paths are very different. It could be argued that the whole trend of Mahler's experience was towards the 'added sixth' chord ending *Das Lied von der Erde*. As a final 'word' such a sound is inconceivable in Bruckner's harmonic vocabulary. Mahler explores and exploits the subjective dimension of his themes; Bruckner, although yielding to the subjective dimension of his own, especially in the slow movements, ends by transcending it. The listener is not troubled by biographical content, or haunted by the ghost of a suppressed programme derived from the composer's reaction to some philosopher or poet. Mahler's themes originate in the maelstrom of his emotional life, a turbulence of anxiety, fantasy and aspiration ever holding them captive. Bruckner works out grand designs from archetypal motives. There are no desperate farewells, no hammer-blows of fate, no philosophical finger-waggings like Zarathustra's Nietzschean warning in Mahler's Third Symphony. To appreciate Bruckner we should simply listen, and perhaps reflect on that tendency in the mind which goes beyond all symbols, images and ideas – as Faust's mind is led by the Feminine at the end of Goethe's drama. It is important to remember that the Mass quotations are not explicit; and there are only very few occasions where Bruckner acknowledges conscious associations, the most obvious being the polka and chorale in the finale of the Third Symphony, the *Totenuhr* ending of the first movement of the Eighth, and the self-quotations at the end of the unfinished Ninth Symphony.

In studying Bruckner's music, we may often be reminded of Beethoven in the opening statements, of Schubert in the lyrical themes and enharmonic modulations, and of Wagner's chromatically-shifting progressions, use of brass and large-scale harmonic conceptions. However, the sound of a Bruckner symphony is unique, and this uniqueness arises from the composer's very individual sense of orchestral colouring. The origin of this has much to do with his training as a contrapuntist and organist. Not only does he contrast blocks of brass and string tone; but he is also very fond of etching fine lines of counterpoint against a shaded string background. A striking example of the first procedure is the massive introduction of the chorale in the finale of the Fifth Symphony (bar 175, Nowak score). Here the theme is given out *fortissimo* on horns, trumpets, trombones and tuba, and followed immediately with a *pianissimo* echo-passage on the upper strings. Less sensational than this, but very characteristic of the way Bruckner's mind works, is the *pianissimo* ending of the exposition of the first movement of the Third Symphony. This is a gentle string chord of F major, romantically coloured by solo horn. Immediately after the double bar, the F major chord is taken up most beautifully by the upper woodwind, the horn again contributing its note. Such changes of colour are synonymous with changes of architectural perspective, subtle or dramatic as the case may be. The 'etching' of a delicate counterpoint above a soft background is heard to most wonderful effect in the recapitulation of the main theme of the first movement of the Fourth Symphony. As horns, and drums tuned to tonic and dominant of the key, state the opening figure against tremolo strings, a solitary flute plays a new, wandering tune rhapsodically above it. There are many such moments throughout Bruckner's symphonies, and they testify to the clarity of his orchestration. Tovey – who once said in an article on Bruckner's Fourth Symphony that, if you want to hear Wagnerian concert music other than a few overtures and the *Siegfried Idyll*, then try Bruckner – gave rise to the assumption that Bruckner's orchestration is modelled on that of Wagner. In fact, it is not, despite the heavy brass scoring, and the *characteristic* 'Bruckner sound' is not Wagner's. Tovey was more to the point when he said that Bruckner's orchestra often sounds like an organ, and could not do so unless it were free of the mistakes of 'the organ-loft composer'. The block contrasts of tone-colour in Bruckner are quite different from the surging torrent of Wagner's full orchestra.

In the first three symphonies Bruckner uses a classical orchestra reinforced with a warm 'filling' of four horns and three trombones. In the Fourth Symphony this solid middle is strengthened and enriched with a bass tuba. In all the later symphonies Bruckner substitutes the instrument specified as contrabass tuba. In addition, he increases the woodwind group to three of each (flutes, oboes, clarinets and bassoons) in the Eighth Symphony, and adds four more horns. In the Eighth and Ninth Symphonies there are eight horns. It is the combination of eight horns, three trumpets, three trombones and contrabass tuba in the last two symphonies which produces a massive quasi-Wagnerian effect, especially when heightened by triple woodwind. When he introduced the tuba, Bruckner was certainly following Wagner's example. What impressed him was the power and reliability of the contrabass tuba in providing a very firm low bass for the horns and brass. The history of the tubas is a complex subject; but it is important to note that the contrabass tuba, introduced into the romantic orchestra by Wagner, is a large instrument with four valves capable of playing very low notes with great facility. This is a true tuba. The instrument which Wagner called a bass-tuba is really a modified horn. This is also true of the tenor tubas used in the slow movement of the Ninth Symphony.

The Textual Problem

Franz Schalk and Ferdinand Löwe were insensitive to the inner spirit of Bruckner's symphonies and the significance of their formal architecture; and it was this insensitivity which lay behind the excisions and rewriting of the composer's work which flawed the first printed editions for which they were responsible. It is very likely that they believed Bruckner was really trying to compose a 'Wagnerian' symphony, and that they were the ones to help him do it. Unfortunately, Bruckner himself opened the door to the confusion which arose even in his lifetime, continued after his death and, incredibly, is still with us. To appreciate this it is first necessary to note the order of the composer's own revisions, which are the main reason for the existence of different performing versions now. The matter is important as these are now vying with one another on the record market.

The First Symphony was composed during 1865–6. This is known as the 'Linz' Symphony in its original form. It was revised in 1868, 1877 and 1884. Nearly twenty-five years later, in Vienna in 1890, Bruckner reworked it; but it is now generally acknowledged that the first version is better in almost every way. The symphony was first performed in Linz in 1868, with the composer conducting.

The Second Symphony was composed during 1871–2, but immediately revised in 1873. Further revisions followed in 1875–6, 1877, 1878–9 and 1891. Bruckner conducted this work in its first performance in 1873.

The Third Symphony exists in three main versions: the first composed during 1872–3, with considerable alterations in 1874; the second during 1876–7, with still further touching-up in 1878; and the third during 1888–9. The first performance in 1877, with Bruckner conducting, was of the second version.

The Fourth Symphony has two main versions, the first composed in 1874, the second during 1878–80. A new Scherzo was added in 1878. The main problem with this work was the finale, which Bruckner reworked a number of times. Richter conducted the first performance in 1881.

The composer's obvious anxiety over the final form of the Second, Third and Fourth Symphonies makes us wonder whether they ever reached a definitive form. They represent a transitional phase of very rapid growth towards maturity, during which

Bruckner wrestled with notes to try and 'discover' exactly that perfection of form which the primary inspiration implied. Unfortunately, however, the composer was not only motivated by aesthetic considerations arising in his own sensibility; he was also influenced by far too many well-meaning suggestions from his friends and pupils, and by demands for cuts made in rehearsal.

Work on the Fifth Symphony, which Bruckner never heard, began in 1875, and the first form was reached in May 1876. There were some revisions of the first two movements in 1877–8; but this work exists in a reasonably final form. The first performance took place in Graz in 1894, under the baton of Franz Schalk.

The Sixth Symphony was composed during 1879–81, and the second and third movements were conducted by Wilhelm Jahn in Vienna in 1883.

Of the Seventh Symphony, also, there is only one version, with the exception of a few alterations, and this was written during 1881–3. Nikisch conducted the first performance in Leipzig in 1884.

The Eighth Symphony has two versions, the first composed during 1884–7, the second during 1889–90. This was first performed by Richter in Vienna in 1892. It is important to remember that it was during this late period that Bruckner turned back to the First Symphony again, and produced the totally unnecessary 'Vienna' version of 1890.

The unfinished Ninth Symphony was begun in 1887, less than a fortnight after completion of the first version of the Eighth, and finished as far as the *Adagio* in 1894. Sketches of the finale have come down to us; but no one has yet presumed to interpret the composer's ultimate intentions by completing them. The composer was actually considering them on the very morning of his death on 11 October 1896. The original version, together with sketches of the finale, was not published until 1934.

The overall position, then, as Bruckner left it is that four symphonies –the Fifth, Sixth, Seventh and Ninth – exist much as the composer originally conceived them; but there are two versions of the First, three of the Second, four of the Third (if we include the fairly substantial alterations of 1874), two of the Fourth and two of the Eighth. The extent of Bruckner's rewriting ranged from details to extensive rescoring. Moreover, Bruckner continuously scrutinised his scores and kept making minor alterations.

In addition to the difficulties arising from the composer's own revisions, the position was further complicated by the editorial interference of Bruckner's own pupils, to whom he entrusted preparation of the printed scores. The overall result was that these published versions, used in performance for many years, do not match Bruckner's manuscripts in either the original or revised forms as left by the composer. It appears that Franz Schalk and Ferdinand Löwe took it upon themselves to rescore Bruckner's music extensively along Wagnerian lines, and to make large cuts. The musical effect thus produced was vastly different from the one intended. This was conclusively revealed in 1932, when the Ninth Symphony was performed for the first time in Bruckner's original version, and again in 1936 with the performance of the original Fifth. The events leading up to these performances are a salutary study in musicology and personal conflict, and were set in motion by a group of scholars[1] who knew that the performing scores did not correspond with the composer's manuscripts. Schalk and Löwe, years after Bruckner's death, protested against the demand for a thorough examination of Bruckner's own scores. Their doubtful motivation, coupled with the fact that the manuscript scores of the Fifth and Ninth Symphonies used by the printer had disappeared without trace, caused a scandal, and spurred on those determined to arrive at the truth of the matter. The momentous outcome was a series of performing editions by Robert Haas and Alfred Orel.

Bruckner himself had eventually realised that once his music had left his hands it was in danger of serious misrepresentation. He had always resisted cuts at rehearsal as far as possible; but when made he had insisted that they should not be carried through into the printed versions. However, many cuts went through, together with the editorial rewriting of his pupils. In an endeavour to preserve his music as he wanted it, Bruckner willed a parcel of his authentic manuscripts to the Court Library in Vienna. These were the main source of the performing versions prepared by Haas and Orel, who also detailed the discrepancies between the originals and the Schalk–Löwe versions.

The aim of Haas to produce a definitive collected edition has not been fulfilled as he planned. In 1945, before his work was done, he was relieved of his post at the Music Department of the Austrian

[1] August Göllerich, Georg Göhler, Max Auer, Alfred Orel and Robert Haas.

National Library. His successor, Leopold Nowak, was also appointed head of the International Bruckner Society, and under Nowak a complete series of miniature study scores has now been issued. Unfortunately, these do not correspond with the performing scores prepared by Haas, which, at any rate until fairly recently, were the ones mainly used by the world's orchestras. Inevitably this confuses the issue for both music-lover and serious student; but for the sake of convenience and uniformity bar-numbers in this book refer to the miniature scores of the International Bruckner Society.

Regrettably, the sense of schism and divided loyalties which first arose from discovery of discrepancies between what Bruckner wrote and what his first editors decided would be 'better' is tending to persist. The editions of Haas were made with a scrupulous regard for authenticity, and with a keen intuitive perception of the workings of Bruckner's mind. The insight shown by Haas far transcends the meddling of Schalk and Löwe who were, after all, entrusted with a sacred task when their master was too ill and tired to see to it himself – the preservation of his work for posterity. It was Haas and Orel, consulting all the material then available to them, who restored the texts and thus enabled the world to appreciate the splendour of Bruckner's music for the first time.

In assessing the claims of musicological truth, a conflict can arise between strict historical accuracy and intuition. Part of the conflict between Haas and Nowak arises from this. In attempting a definitive final and universally acceptable version, Nowak is a scrupulous editor, his concern being strict adherence to the available data. Haas, likewise scrupulous, has come to know Bruckner's mind so well that he has here and there restored cuts which Bruckner did in fact appear to sanction, confident that in a more enlightened climate of musical understanding Bruckner would have wished this. A case of this arises especially in connection with the Eighth Symphony.

The present position is that a set of miniature scores now exists which, bearing the imprint of the International Bruckner Society, is intended to be definitive. These are largely based on the original work of Haas; but in addition they contain a number of further editorial modifications made in the name of musicological accuracy. It may be doubted, especially in the case of the Third Symphony, whether the Nowak version would always be found acceptable by the composer. The editorial work is also being extended to the performing scores, with the very practical consequence for both student and record enthusiast that both Haas and Nowak versions are competing for the favour of conductors and recording companies. Fortunately, it is now becoming the practice to indicate on the record covers which version is being used. The listener who prefers his Bruckner to sound as the composer really intended must therefore use his powers of critical discrimination to the utmost. In this he will be substantially helped by the fine study of the symphonies made by Robert Simpson[1] and the biographical and critical survey written by Erwin Doernberg,[2] to both of which the present writer also makes grateful acknowledgement. Doernberg discusses the editorial problem at length, and Simpson, when necessary, clarifies the musical situation as between different versions. There are also many important studies of Bruckner and his music in German, notably by Robert Haas, Max Auer, Alfred Orel, August Göllerich and Ernst Kurth.

The Early Years

Bruckner was late in taking up the full-time profession of music. Following his father, a schoolmaster at Ansfelden, he wished to be a teacher, and eventually became one at the small village of Windhaag where, however, he was also required to work in the fields. At Windhaag he played in a local dance group for a time, no doubt gaining experience and impressions projected later in the scherzi of his symphonies. He had already become proficient on the organ and had become acquainted with the St Florian Krisman organ during time spent as a pupil-chorister at the religious foundation. Work in the fields accorded ill with his musical pursuits. Eventually he was sent to Kronstorf, near Steyr, where he was able to take up theoretical studies with Leopold von Zenetti. In September 1845 he went to St Florian as a teacher. Bruckner's life, especially in the early and impressionable years, revolved round the Church, and he absorbed profound influences from his study of liturgical music. The culmination of such influences, fused with

[1] Robert Simpson. *The Essence of Bruckner* (London, 1967).
[2] Erwin Doernberg, *The Life and Symphonies of Anton Bruckner* (London, 1960).

increasing musical aspirations, took him to Linz in 1855 as organist of the cathedral. In July of that year he had been accepted as a pupil of Simon Sechter, the contrapuntist with whom Schubert had once considered lessons. Thanks to the insight of Bishop Rudigier of Linz, he was allowed ample opportunity to avail himself of Sechter's teaching in Vienna. Bishop Rudigier was a benign and inspirational influence upon Bruckner during a time of stress and slowly crystallising aspiration, and he actively encouraged him in his creative work.

The influence of Sechter during the years 1855–61 was considerable. He was a severe disciplinarian, and subjected his students to a grilling in harmony and counterpoint, double-counterpoint, canon and fugue which modern music students would doubtless consider dry, acidulated and unnecessary. Bruckner passed all the tests and examinations Sechter set him, and emerged from his studentship a master of traditional techniques, with his intellectual prowess fully recognised by the establishment of the Vienna Conservatory after he had amazed a panel of experts with fugal improvisation on the organ.

The training with Sechter was, however, only one aspect of the young composer's studentship. Sechter insisted upon exercises only, with a total 'blackout' on free composition. Under Otto Kitzler, a younger man than Bruckner, steeped in the ethos of Wagner and Liszt, he studied orchestration and sonata-form during the years 1861–3. Through Kitzler his musical sensibilities were brought up to date and educated through contact with the contemporary musical atmosphere.

The influences which played upon Bruckner, especially through Sechter and Kitzler, explain to some extent the fascinating blend of contrapuntal virility, monumental form and orchestral colour in his music. [1] Factors already mentioned – the influence of the Mass, Wagner's music and the organ – were disciplined and bound together by a mind bent on achieving mastery of all the fundamental techniques of composition. Ultimately all the elements of Bruckner's musical background were sublimated in rigorous and abstract structures.

---

[1] Egon Wellesz sees a parallel between Bruckner and another famous Austrian contrapuntist, Fux, in that both combined a characteristic Austrian warmth of feeling with contrapuntal mastery. See E. Wellesz, *Fux* (Oxford, 1965).

It is interesting that both Mahler and Bruckner included lyrical self-quotation in their symphonic works, Mahler leaning heavily upon his *Wunderhorn* songs, and Bruckner upon his Masses. In the Masses there is a generic consistency, reflected in a certain stylistic orientation of the symphonies. In the Second Symphony, for example, there are substantial quotations from the F minor Mass in the *Adagio* and finale. In general, the influence of Mass upon symphony is observable in sectional construction, melodic patterns which sound as though they could easily be made to fit portions of Latin texts, and in the way ascending and descending figures are used in climactic passages. The listener may explore this interesting subject at his leisure aided by the excellent recordings now available. What matters most, however, is the symphonic transmutation of liturgical influences and fragments brought about through the abstract processes of Bruckner's musical thinking.

SYMPHONY 'O'

THE OVERTURE IN G MINOR

Something of the alchemical fusion of influences can be sensed in three early works, the 'Student Symphony' in F minor (1863), Symphony '0' and the Overture in G minor. The so-called 'Zero' Symphony was completed in 1869; but it was most likely begun before the official First Symphony. Its first movement at once awakens memories of Beethoven's Ninth, and despite the fact that it substitutes atmospheric vibration for a strong thematic opening – the symphony has been criticised for its lack of an unambiguous first subject – the work as a whole is an impressive piece of writing which did not deserve the composer's own harsh judgment upon it. Bruckner was unfortunately far too much influenced by his desire to satisfy influential musical authorities. Otto Dessoff, conductor of the Court Opera in Vienna, had been one of Bruckner's examiners at the Vienna Conservatory. On being shown the score, he asked: 'Where is the main subject?' For the sensitive and too humble composer this must have seemed like a douche of cold water; so the symphony was set aside. Dessoff was also bleakly unhelpful on a later occasion when Bruckner submitted the Second Symphony to the Vienna Philharmonic.

Symphony '0' is well worth hearing, and is of special interest in that it contains anticipations of later symphonies and quotations from the Masses in E minor and F minor, a setting of the *Ave Maria* of 1861 and an early Mass in B flat of 1854 (see p. 9n.). In the first movement, Bruckner gets to grips with what later proved to be his central symphonic concept – a process of structural unfolding from nebulous beginnings. The opening figuration is a clear indication of the impression made by Beethoven's last symphony, and it clearly foreshadows the opening of Bruckner's Third Symphony in the same key, D minor. This strong Beethoven influence must have resulted from the experience of first hearing the Ninth Symphony in 1866, in which case the first movement of Symphony '0' must either have been composed after the official First Symphony, or else reconstructed under the dominating impact of Beethoven's opening statement.

Of special interest is the vigorous Overture in G minor, which dated from Bruckner's study with Kitzler but remained unpublished until 1921. It is far superior to the two military band marches and the four orchestral pieces of 1862. The Overture is virtually a symphonic first movement. Its clean, sinewy lines and incisive scoring make it a fitting prelude to the nine great symphonies.

It is composed on the French model, with a powerful *Adagio* introduction. The opening statement has a classical symmetry:

Ex.1

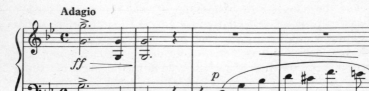

The climbing figure soon leads, however, into an intense falling chromatic passage, gradually subsiding into hushed dominant expectancy. The *Allegro* moves off briskly on the strings, with the main figure supported by a running figure on violas. Continuation of the opening theme picks up the falling motive from the *Adagio* and initiates a climactic extension where rushing semiquavers alternate with an ascending figure related to the cello and viola figures in Ex. 1. Very characteristically, the pressure is then relaxed for a second subject. This is the part of a symphonic exposition where the composer liked to introduce a quiet, contrasting, song-like melody which he called the *Gesangsperiode*:

Ex.2

The woodwind commentary on this which follows immediately is again characteristic. The harmony modulates chromatically before wind instruments take up the falling seventh (*x*) and with it shape the rest of the exposition against an energetic string background.

Development is terse, dramatic and forceful in working out chromatic implications contained in the slow introduction. Three trombones, trumpets and drums play a full-blooded role in the middle of the tutti as the orchestra pounds away *ff* on the ascending figure of Ex. 1. The opening theme of the *Allegro* then comes in for extended and imaginative treatment with woodwind and horns answering one another.

Recapitulation is ushered in quietly, following chromatic ascent to submediant harmony with the three trombones again forming a solid middle block in close 6/3 harmony. The *Gesangsperiode* reappears in an altered and shortened form and is immediately followed by the coda, initiated *ff* with two explosive chords. Chromatic tension is increased dramatically until the music slows down to a cadence in the home key. Then, against a quiet string background, a solo horn quotes the theme of the *Allegro* for the last time. It is an evocative moment of romantic feeling just before the gathering momentum of the tutti precipitates the closing bars. The Overture ends with a strong plagal cadence and a *tierce de Picardie*. It is a splendid piece of writing, deserving more performances than it receives.

SYMPHONY NO. I IN C MINOR

In 1890, when Bruckner revised his 'Linz' Symphony, he had moved beyond the intellectual climate and feeling of the work, and so could 'hear' it only with a mind attuned to the vast structures of the later symphonies. We should beware of following him in this. The original version has its own integrity and internal logical consistency. It cannot be considered a youthful work: after all, Bruckner was forty-one when he wrote it. The thematic material, development and overall structure are the achievement of a composer of genius whose intellect and imagination are fully awake.

The *Allegro* opens with a stumping march-rhythm set in motion by the lower strings. Above this, violins give out a rather dour, tightly-knit and dotted-note theme marked by reiterated minor seconds:

Ex.3

These are emphasised by interjections on the horn. Other instruments join in, and a sudden uprushing scale precipitates an early climax as the chord of the dominant seventh side-slips to A flat. The climax subsides quickly in a transitional passage, and then a sweet descending woodwind phrase, joined by solo horn, introduces the second subject in the key of E flat:

Ex.4

This is the characteristic *Gesangsperiode*, a theme of meditative beauty. The main melody of one of Bruckner's *Gesangsperioden* is usually accompanied by a counterpoint which is itself melodically interesting, if not actually imitative of the theme. In this case the rocking figure marked is important towards the end of the movement, where the strings use it to build up tremendous momentum. The melody is heard first on violins and subsequently on cellos. Almost immediately afterwards tension mounts rapidly. A new and powerfully rhythmic sub-theme is made the basis of a *fortissimo* sequence which explodes into a splendid third main theme. The trombones stand out magnificently here. This great theme is the climax of the exposition:

Ex.5

Observe the important minor second C flat–B flat. As the new theme dies away, it yields to a calm six-bar phrase (woodwind and horn answered by strings) ending the exposition serenely in the relative major key.

The closing group initiates development; but it is not long before the tutti builds up again. The pressure of Ex. 5 is pervasive, although the theme is not restated literally. More important are the reiterated minor seconds which illuminate the connection of Ex. 5 with the opening theme. Eventually the rhythm of Ex. 3 returns and is developed. Prior to recapitulation the dominant key, previously avoided in the exposition by the sudden side-slip to A flat, appears for a few moments to prepare the home key. This is sounded by a *pianissimo* drum roll accompanying Ex. 3 – a splendid effect. The *Gesangsperiode* is heard again; but the triumphant Ex. 5 is not. It thus takes its place as a massive centrepiece in the movement, and its position and function bring about a change of emphasis within the traditional sonata-form structure. In the Vienna version, Bruckner brings back Ex. 4 in the coda for a final grand statement, or rather mis-statement, for it is certainly a gross artistic lapse. By this time its function is exhausted and a further appearance, especially on the trumpet, introduces an element of brazen ugliness. The Linz version is content to ram home the rhythmic momentum of the dotted-note figure with which the movement opens.

The slow movement emerges only slowly from subterranean broodings. Strings play hesitant, chromatic fragments, significantly reiterating the interval of the minor second. Not until the twentieth bar do flutes offer relief in a sequential diatonic passage. The first theme, presented as a duo above a flowing arpeggio accompaniment, emerges in the thirtieth bar, apparently in B flat; but this key is revealed as a dominant enhancement of E flat. The first sweep of this lovely melody ends with an upturned phrase, like many a theme of Mozart. After a brief climax, the time changes to 3/4 and another melody appears. This second main tune is the basis of an extended middle section, eventually yielding to a return of the opening passage, now considerably rescored with the accompaniment of running semiquavers built up in the central part of the movement. The first theme does not reappear in its original form, although the opening phrase is heard. This leads quickly to a final climax, after which the movement ends quietly with ascending and descending arpeggios.

The *Adagio* seems to be in ternary form, and could be so considered were it not for the significant opening matter, later recapitulated in modified form. This establishes the first recognisable melody at bar 30 as a *secondary group*. The second theme proper, seemingly presented as the centre section of a ternary structure, is really where a formal development would have occurred in a sonata-form movement. The overall form is thus more complex than it sounds, and any temptation to pin firm labels on it should be resisted. The last remark applies to a great many Bruckner movements. His conception of sonata-form, and of symphonic form in general, is far from orthodox, despite the deceptive simplicity of the traditional four-movement layout. In Bruckner's music each thematic group is a growing point, and its organic relationship with other groups can be subtle and profound. The developmental and interlocking procedures cannot be subsumed in neat formal categories.

However, in his scherzi the composer does follow a basic ternary pattern. A common error, perpetuated on record sleeves, refers less to form than to style. It is quite true that in some scherzi Bruckner adopts the rhythms and much of the spirit of Austrian country dances which he used to play on his fiddle at Windhaag; but it is absurd to assume that the moment he came to write a scherzo Bruckner was instantly hypnotised by the image of jolly woodcutters jumping about in leather trousers. Bruckner's Austrianism reveals itself most beautifully in the middle sections of his ternary scherzi; and in the enclosing outer sections there is undoubtedly a rumbustious rural flavour. In the main, however, and even in this First Symphony, the composer transcends the peasant image in music of energy and power. It is the drive, the whirling spin, the tremendous momentum which remain dominant impressions. Like Beethoven, Bruckner destroys the regular periodicity of the reiterated 3/4 bars to stamp the movement with hurtling dynamism. This is very apparent in the scherzo of the First Symphony. The trio is in marked contrast and contains many beautiful moments reminiscent of Josef Lanner, not the least of which is the delightful flat sixth in the waltz-like horn melody.

The finale is all hard-driving energy, initiated with a furious dotted-note theme. A second theme is also vigorous but less aggressive. The racing semiquavers return with a third figure at bar 58 and are maintained, ff, until they suddenly end with a dramatic pause. The calm closing phrase, introduced by the wind, is based upon double augmentation of the violin figure A flat–G–F–E flat. A further felicitous touch is a reference in this closing group to the dotted-note figure in the second bar of the first theme.

Development opens with soft, meditative consideration of this same figure before the energetic drive of the movement starts again at bar 111. Again the dotted-note rhythm is prominent as the tutti moves to a climax – a shattering, unprepared blaze of E major – after which it collapses rapidly to a whisper of horns and drum-taps. Another pause ushers in development of the second theme with free inversion (bar 163) and an energetic contrapuntal texture which hacks its way remorselessly towards material from the third theme. Tension mounts as the finale drives on towards recapitulation at bar 273. The opening challenge is sounded in a triumphant C major; but C minor soon reasserts its dominance. However, the brief flash of C major is like a sudden gleam of sunlight behind storm-clouds; the listener senses that everything is opening out towards the major key. The expected and conclusive affirmation of C major is made with a shortened statement of the second subject. The key signature changes definitively as three rising steps C–D–E natural pave the way for the splendid trumpet theme which ends the movement. The final chords are rammed home with the dotted-note rhythm from the first theme.

The First Symphony has an atmosphere all its own, and is stylistically different from its successors. It should not, therefore, be regarded as an early attempt to write something bigger or better. Nor should canons of judgment and interpretation proper to the later works be projected upon it.

SYMPHONY NO. 2 IN C MINOR

We may often wonder at the psychological burden of genius, at the reaction of human personality to the inward pressure of works yet unborn. After completing the First Symphony, Bruckner suffered a nervous breakdown, the contributory causes of which may well have originated in a recurring lack of self-confidence. It is not impossible that religious faith temporarily failed him. There is always a negative factor in faith, as if doubt itself is the thrust-block from which faith takes its strength. We cannot know how far, if at all, this applied to the mental crisis of 1867. The composer overcame it, assisted by the ministrations of a priest sent to help him by Bishop Rudigier of Linz. The inner victory is certainly reflected in the great Mass in F minor, composed in 1867–8 and revised in 1881. The mysticism of this work does not, like Beethoven's, place it outside the limits of Christian orthodoxy. Bruckner's Mass is Roman Catholic church music, testifying to the convictions of a man whose religious needs were wholly served by the Church.

After writing the Mass, Bruckner was invited to England in 1871 to play the Willis organ in the Albert Hall. It was in London that he started work on the Second Symphony. With this Bruckner entered upon a difficult transitional period, from which he did not completely emerge until the composition of the Fifth Symphony. For critical convenience it is therefore possible to adopt a very rough threefold classification. The First Symphony can be set on its own as a work of early maturity. The Second, Third and Fourth Symphonies (1871–4) then fall into a second massive transitional group. The Fifth, Sixth, Seventh, Eighth and Ninth, each unique and splendid masterpieces requiring separate consideration, constitute the final phase of creative activity covering the years 1875–94. Nothing so naïve as the traditional three-period development is intended by this division. In any case, the position is vastly complicated by the revisions of the earlier symphonies which overlap into the years of the last works.

Dr Simpson believes that the Second, the Third and the finale of the Fourth Symphonies never reached, in Bruckner's estimation, a definitive form. Two factors may be relevant here: on the one hand, a habit of self-criticism carried to excess, which prevented the composer from leaving anything alone, especially with friends advising him to write something simpler; on the other, a genuine realisation that during the period represented by these works his mind was exploring vast new seas of symphonic experience, and at first genuinely unable to charter and finally grasp in their innermost nature the forms he discovered (for composition is essentially a kind of discovery). He is like an explorer who discovers more treasure than he can carry away.

Both Haas and Nowak used the 1877 version of the Second Symphony in preparing their editions. Haas, however, restored parts from the end of the first and second movements and finale. In noting this, Erwin Doernberg says that no conductor with a true feeling for Bruckner would ever dream of leaving these sections unplayed. Nowak, however, thinks differently, and in the Bruckner Society score issued in 1965 he accuses Haas of confusing the first and 1877 versions. He therefore cuts out what Haas considered to be in the essential spirit of the work. It is important to remember here that Bruckner was much disturbed by contemporary reaction to the symphony. Herbeck, one of the panel of examiners who had acclaimed Bruckner's skill and knowledge at the examination in 1861, turned against it. So did Otto Dessoff. The general feeling was that Bruckner should simplify his conceptions and tone everything down to more acceptable classical proportions. In his nervous anxiety to obey the classical canon, Bruckner wrestled endlessly with notes to achieve a standard which others would consider acceptable.

But it is easy to see that what really upset the composer's critics, and indeed the Vienna Philharmonic Orchestra, was the scale and depth of the music – an impact which persisted despite all cuts and changes. Bruckner himself hired the orchestra, who became enthusiastic in performance. Yet they would not accept the dedication. Neither, in any real sense, would Liszt, who lost the score, which subsequently found its way back to Bruckner through a third party. Then Hanslick and the Brahms faction turned sour. After performing the work once more in 1894, the orchestra shelved it for close on twenty years. The great centre of European music has not always dealt kindly with its greatest musicians, and Vienna's romantic associations – largely dependent in the popular mind upon its delightful tradition of light music – should not blind us to this fact.

The opening of the symphony is arresting. Notice particularly the ambiguous submediant effect, with C minor tonality outlined by the falling horn arpeggio G–E flat–C (Ex. 6 opposite). This is followed, after extension, by the second subject, a beautiful *Gesangsperiode* in E flat. A third subject is then introduced above a repetitive unison bass figure continued for more than fifty bars

$$(\; \text{♩} \; \text{♫} \text{♩} \; \text{♫} \;)$$

This persistent rhythm is complicated by trumpets entering at bar 122 with a variant

$$(\; \text{♩.} \quad \text{♪♩.} \; \text{♪♩} \;)$$

of what has come to be known as the 'Bruckner rhythm'

$$(\; \text{♩} \; \text{♩} \; \text{♩} \text{♩} \text{♩} \;)$$

because of its prominence in the Third, Fourth and Eighth Symphonies.

In development, the thematic material is most interestingly explored, especially the opening theme (Ex. 6). The whole section is a contrapuntal *tour de force*, rich in allusions to all the main ideas, and constructed with an ear for expansive modulation. Particularly striking is the excursion into G flat, which opens up a gentle rocking passage with woodwind and horns outlined against a modulating background of strings. The repetitive figure accompanying the third theme now comes into view as an independent country tune on violins in counterpoint with wind. This rises to a climax which in turn yields, after reference to the second theme, to recapitulation at bar 320. The coda is massive, and heavy with a clear reference (as many writers have pointed out) to the chromatic figure stalking through the coda of the first movement of Beethoven's Ninth Symphony. The final battery of sound hammering home the last chords is preceded by wistful reference to the first subject.

The beautiful slow movement has the peace and tranquillity of a mountain mirrored in a Lakeland tarn. The form is a simple ABABA. Its first theme (*A*) has a broad, majestic sweep (Ex. 7) and is heard three times. An alternating theme consists of a gentle, chorale-like passage, introduced pizzicato, with a lovely horn phrase in counterpoint. This is immediately repeated with

Ex.7

sensuously enhanced scoring, bassoons and clarinets being added to
the horn melody, and legato violin arpeggios to the pizzicato
chorale phrases. Return to the main theme is by way of a
chromatically ascending horn passage, slightly odd in this context.
A is now heard with richer scoring, and after it has died away to *pp*
and a pause *B* reappears in much the same layout as before. The
final broadened version of *A* leads to a quotation from the *Benedictus*
of the Mass in F minor (bar 180 in the miniature score). After this
the movement fades to a hushed conclusion. In the first version the
horn plays a prominent role in the closing bars with a *pp* A flat
arpeggio. Nowak prints this as an alternative ending in the
miniature score, the 'official' version substituting clarinet, which is
technically easier if not so romantically evocative.

The scherzo is charged with dynamic impetus, full of rhythmic
tricks and imaginative modulation; but it is likely to be the poetic,
dreamy trio which lingers in the memory. Here Bruckner shows
himself well aware not only of the poetry of Austria's dance music
but also of Schubert's inspired enharmonic modulations.

The finale busies itself immediately with a descending-scale
figure which awakens echoes of the opening of the symphony.
However, this passage seems designed mainly to initiate
momentum for the *fortissimo* main theme:

Ex.8

Such a tremendous outburst of energy seems powerful enough to
precipitate a hectic and extended structure rather in the manner of
the finale of Schubert's 'Great' C major Symphony. However, the

headlong rush is guillotined at bar 51. After a pause the busy opening figure returns, this time leading to a dominant seventh in D flat. Another pause – followed this time by a graceful theme in the totally unprepared key of A major. This is the *Gesangsperiode*, contrasting remarkably here with what has gone before. It is easy to see that such music must have been a shock to classically-nurtured sensibilities. The song-section makes its way deviously towards orthodox tonal orientation in E flat. When Bruckner feels that this has lasted long enough, the main theme (Ex. 8) is brought back in E flat major (bar 148). This second statement is forced up to *fff* before it is again brusquely axed. By now the intuitive listener hearing the work for the first time will have realised that this is the theme on which the symphony *must* end. The overall form of the movement is complex – one might almost say a collision between sonata and rondo. The effect is of successive attempts to make a breakthrough to a triumphant and absolutely decisive C major, on the basis of Ex. 8. To this end the theme is used like a battering-ram, and momentum is built up by the opening figure referring to the first movement. Over and above all generalisations about sonata-form, rondo and so on, there is a powerful psychological effect inviting description in more picturesque language. After each rising wave the music falls back into bars of silence and quiet contemplation – a very characteristic feature of Bruckner's music. One of the most telling examples of this comes at bar 197. After a few moments of complete silence the strings usher in a hushed quotation in G flat from the Mass in F minor. This announces the end of the exposition, formally reached when the Mass quotation modulates to E flat.

Development and recapitulation are exciting. Best of all is the breakthrough (*fff*) to C major (bar 680), finally dispelling the haunting C minor quavers which dominated both the beginning of the finale and the opening of the symphony.

Hanslick's hostility
The Third and Fourth Symphonies

SYMPHONY NO. 3 IN D MINOR

Eduard Hanslick wrote of the Third Symphony that it defied understanding, that its poetic meaning was never revealed, and that its principle of continuity was elusive and made it difficult to grasp. In his criticism, printed in the *Wiener Zeitung* on 16 December 1877, he accused Bruckner of confusing Beethoven with Wagner and finally submitting to Wagnerian influence. To understand this reaction – which is not wholly uncommon today – we must look to the music itself and to some important historical and artistic considerations.

Hanslick, critic of the *Wiener Zeitung* since 1848, author of a famous treatise *On the Beautiful in Music* (1854), was made professor of musical history and aesthetics at the University of Vienna in 1861. Brucknerians will not lightly forgive the misery he inflicted on the composer by ceaseless denigration of his music during his lifetime; but for all that he was not such a superficial critic as Tovey made him out to be in his discussion of the Fourth Symphony.[1] The main trouble with Hanslick was that his musical sensibilities were formed by, and rested only on, the classics of the Viennese School. He had no knowledge of, and presumably no interest in, the adventurous music of Berlioz, for example, and the romantic tradition generally, and did not feel it his duty to educate himself in contemporary developments. He detested Wagner, in the beginning mainly for political reasons arising from the 1848 revolution in Vienna when they were on opposite sides. Prior to that, relations had been reasonably cordial. The developing personal animosity was fostered by the caricature of himself as Beckmesser in *Die Meistersinger*, and also by some genuine convictions about the nature of music and the significance of musical experience.

To Hanslick 'the essence of music is sound in motion'. The main thesis of *Vom Musikalisch-Schönen* is that beauty is a property of a structure of sounds: it has nothing to do with persons, places, things, events or ideas. Armed with this view, which found support amongst lovers of traditional classicism, Hanslick championed Brahms, the supposed true heir of Beethoven, against Wagner and his conception of *Gesamtkunstwerk*, which put forward a passionate plea for the synthesis of all the arts with philosophy, and thus led to a symbolic interpretation of music. Theorists opposed to Hanslick, aflame with romantic ideas which they felt to be abundantly justified in the work of Berlioz, Wagner, Liszt and others, believed that the sensuous structure of musical sounds could indeed express

[1] *Essays in Musical Analysis*, II, pp. 70–1 (Oxford, 1935).

emotions, ideas, images, character, feeling, mystical apprehension and so on. Thus the art and theory of *Tonsatz*, the structure of sound in motion, becomes a musical vehicle of the flux of the inner life.

What about Bruckner? Bruckner brought down calamity upon his own head. Entranced by the sound of Wagner's music, whilst remaining totally indifferent to the theory of *Gesamtkunstwerk*, he dedicated the Third Symphony to him without the remotest idea what adverse consequences would follow. Wagner accepted the dedication, and always referred to the symphony afterwards as the one with the trumpet, on account of the powerful opening theme, which strongly appealed to him. The source of this appeal is obvious enough if we compare Bruckner's archetypal theme with the opening motive of *The Flying Dutchman*:

Ex.9

(a) Bruckner

(b) Wagner

Both figures spring from the D minor arpeggio; Bruckner's falls, Wagner's ascends. In fact, Bruckner's climbs back again and seems to reach a point of finality which poses problems in symphonic development. The apparent significance of the dedication to Wagner was not lost on the supporters of the Hanslick–Brahms party or the student friends of Bruckner. To the Brahmsians Bruckner had sealed himself with the abhorred sign. To his adherents, he had proclaimed his Wagnerian sympathies and discipleship.

In fact, Bruckner was a symphonist preoccupied with the

problems of large-scale form and fascinated by the sound of Wagner's orchestra. His music is free of just those aspects Hanslick opposed in Wagner. He did not 'violate music with words'. Nor is the unfolding of his symphonic procedures 'monotonous, measureless and enervating' to anyone who understands them. Nor, again, did Bruckner compose themes as musical symbols with dramatic intent. The various Mass-quotations may have had private meaning for himself; but one can enjoy Bruckner without knowing they are there. Bruckner's inner life was not married to some idealistic programme, nor is it openly proclaimed in non-musical associations. Rather is its spiritual quality 'shown' in some elusive factor beyond the power of verbal description. It was Bruckner's great misfortune to have become embroiled in the Hanslick–Wagner battle when he was grappling with problems of symphonic form, problems which were wholly abstract and had their roots in the fundamentals of *Tonsatz*.

Unfortunately, in this Third Symphony, which became an unwitting symbol of Bruckner's 'Wagnerianism', there are problems which the composer never satisfactorily resolved in any of his revisions. Moreover, by seizing on the continuity issue, Hanslick had for once put his finger on a valid point. But this issue was further confounded by the cuts made at the first performance. What Hanslick heard was a transitional work hacked about without any real insight into problems of balance. What he *thought* he heard was a long-winded and disjointed pastiche of Beethoven and Wagner served up by a nervous little rustic who had had the temerity in 1874 to apply for a teaching post at the University – an application which Hanslick had repeatedly opposed on grounds of his lack of qualification. (Bruckner unqualified!)

As it happens, Bruckner's Third Symphony is now one of the most popular with listeners new to his music; yet it has some shortcomings which become apparent in comparison with later works. Splendid though the main theme is, it may be questioned whether Bruckner ever manages to do much with it. After its initial appearance, the music seems to hang back uncertainly until the arrival of a second powerful figure at bar 31, stated twice – the first time in unison, the second in dramatic harmony. The new theme has two contrasting sections, the second leading to recapitulation of the first group in the dominant (A major). Commentators invariably point out that this reverses Beethoven's procedure in the opening of the Ninth Symphony. However, Bruckner's movement achieves nothing like the organic growth of Beethoven's; yet he creates an impression of immense power held in reserve. Indeed, this may point to one of the weaknesses of the symphony, which never gives full and satisfying expression to the force encapsulated in the opening bars. The final statement of the main theme, heard at the end of the finale, is too short and inadequately prepared.

The second-subject group opens with a *Gesangsperiode* in F (bar 101) combining two figures contrapuntally, in which we hear the familiar Bruckner rhythm. This is an appropriate moment to remark on the vertical depth of Bruckner's thematic ideas, generated by arpeggios, and often filling a space of two octaves or more. There can be no doubt that this leaping and plunging through a deep vertical compass (compare, for example, the opening theme of the Seventh Symphony, Ex. 20) exerts a 'spatial' drag upon the time-spread of the formal process. It is as if the music tends ever to expand in a spatial sense; and the more powerful this tendency is, the more time is required to work out its formal implications. In fact the third version, the basis of Nowak's study score, is arguably too short for its thematic content, especially in the finale, which is truncated by the omission of important material.

New material appears at bar 127 with thematic interest in the cellos, the three-plus-two rhythm persisting throughout. Another monumental figure appears in unison at bar 171, and this ushers in a related chorale figure at bar 199, with violin accompaniment derived from the opening of the movement. After all this thematic exposition, the composer possibly feels that his lines of communication are beginning to be overstretched, so he introduces the main theme in canon between trombones and horns. After this the exposition comes to a gentle close with long slow chords in F major.

Development growing from these quiet sounds tackles the problem of the main theme (Ex. 9a). What shall be done with it? How must it unfold to release its power? Bruckner's procedure is static. He turns it upside down and repeats the canon, this time between strings, horn and woodwind. Inverted and original forms answer one another. The impression grows that this fine theme is imprisoned by its own harmonic space: it will not *move*. Much finer music is heard with the revised development based upon the second theme (bar 321). Trombones and horns add a diminished fragment of the opening trumpet theme. This leads to a great climax at bar 341, in which the main theme is declaimed *fff* in a manner suggesting recapitulation (which it is not), and this precipitates extended comment on the all-important first three notes. When this has crashed to a pause with a solitary drum roll, there is an episodic return of the *Gesangsperiode* followed, very quaintly, by a reference to the opening theme of the Second Symphony (bar 415). What private thought prompted this reminiscence?

Recapitulation is shortened. When the coda begins with a drum-roll analogous to that introducing the recapitulation, Bruckner reveals his deep interest in the chromatic bass initiating the coda of the first movement of Beethoven's Ninth Symphony. The mood and atmosphere are similar.

The second movement is much altered in the third version. The opening theme has a classical sound; but it is followed up in a late-romantic way. At bar 21 Bruckner quotes a Mozartian phrase previously used in his *Ave Maria* for chorus and organ (1856) and a piano piece, 'Remembrance' (1868). The scherzo contains a delightful trio revealing his love and early experience of Austria's dance music. Both Bruckner and Mahler allowed poetic fancy great freedom in such movements.

The finale is complex, and returns to the formal and developmental problems posed by the main thematic content of the first movement. It is in many respects Bruckner's least satisfactory symphonic movement in that it alternately generates and destroys momentum. The cyclic effect intended thus degenerates into a desperate attempt to confirm that the main theme of the symphony is what the symphony is all about.

Violins begin with a hectic chromatic figure, and the first theme, as might be expected, is related to Ex. 9(a). The second theme, a violin polka, is introduced in A major with an accompanying chorale on horns and brass. This is one of the few cases in a Bruckner symphony where the composer makes explicit reference to a non-musical event. Apparently he was walking past the Schottenring in the late evening when he heard the music of a ball. Nearby in the Sühnhaus lay the body of a famous architect. Bruckner was struck by the contrast, and moved to a little melancholy philosophising. The story is told by his friend and biographer August Göllerich. Certainly the unusual juxtaposition of themes gives musical structure to the story, and in this moment

Bruckner approaches Mahler's conception of symphony as a 'world'.

A third and very powerful theme is introduced *ff* in syncopated unisons at bar 155, and immediately repeated, after which the exposition ends characteristically with sustained chords. It is interesting that Liszt liked to end piano pieces with similar liturgical-sounding progressions; but one feels that with him it was a self-conscious gesture and not, as with Bruckner, a spontaneous and natural cadential procedure.

From here onwards the movement tends to misfire, especially in the third version. Violins return to the opening quaver patterns, and the music moves to the dominant of C major when the main trumpet theme (Ex. 9a) makes a premature and disastrous appearance.[1] This has the effect of arresting momentum. There is a long rest, the chorale theme returns without the polka counterpoint and then, in the third version, is repeated *with* the polka, in A flat. In the second version, which is better, there is some development of the first theme here, and it is very much needed. By this time the second-subject group is beginning to sound tedious. It is a relief when the third theme returns to instil more energy and drive. The final climax arrives at bar 451 (third version) with emphatic repetitions of Ex. 9(a) augmented in the tonic major. The sound of the closing bars is magnificent; but the triumphant fanfares leave the lingering impression of a premature summons.

SYMPHONY NO. 4 IN E FLAT

One has only to study the beautiful first movement of the Fourth Symphony, traditionally known as 'The Romantic', to feel a much more confident and steady hand in charge of formal development. The opening bars are shown in Ex. 10 overleaf. They seem to be based on just that kind of harmonic inspiration which sometimes happens spontaneously during ruminative piano improvisation before the mind registers exactly what the hands are doing. The horn call is first heard against a shimmering string tremolo. The flat submediant note (C flat), which gives such haunting beauty to the symphony, is echoed immediately in the accompanying harmony at the eighth bar, and its implications are followed through in the

[1] See Robert Simpson's dramatic and entertaining account of this movement, *op cit.*, pp. 75–80.

Ex.10

Bewegt, nicht zu schnell

succeeding harmony. The return to tonic E flat major harmony at the seventeenth bar confirms the mood of almost unearthly peace. After this, woodwind and horns open an antiphonal dialogue, passing through veils of Schubertian harmony. It is one of those wonderful Brucknerian melodies which unfold 'spatially'. Until the familiar rhythm appears at bar 43 it is not possible to determine the speed at which events are moving. Compared with this music, the first movement of the Third Symphony seems somewhat 'wooden'. The difference between the formal inevitability of the Fourth and the irregular flow of the Third Symphony arises from the nature of the main themes. That of the Third, magnificent gesture though it is, makes its point all at once – it is a 'dogmatic' utterance and its reiteration opens no doors to progressive musical discussion. In the Fourth, on the contrary, the opening theme invites an infinite expansion. The difference arises from the expansive developmental implications of romantic harmony. Bruckner's 'Wagner theme' is solidly encased in the structure of a single triad, outlined, of course, by the harmonic implications of I–V–I. The Fourth also asserts this primary relation (B flat–E flat); but the C flat enhancement and the magical chord at the seventh bar completely dissolve the harmonic and thematic fixation of V–I despite the gravitational pull of the underlying tonic pedal. After this, anything can happen. A wonderful spectrum of harmonic relationships has been opened up, and Bruckner proceeds to unfold some of the almost infinite possibilities in what follows.

There are some especially beautiful moments at the end of the development (bar 333) when strings play a passage based on an augmented form of a theme first heard in the *Gesangsperiode* on violas:

Ex.11

Immediately after this the movement begins to recapitulate, with a flute playing a new counter-melody above the horn call of Ex. 10. This is later taken up by the cellos. At the end of the movement the horn-calls are heard again and again – wonderful sounds stirring the mind and heart of those who love the country which produced them.

The slow movement is a march with melancholy and Schubertian overtones, full of subtleties which repay close listening. From C minor, the key of the march, Bruckner moves to B flat for the scherzo. This is all hard-hitting energy, initiated by electrifying horn-calls rapping out the composer's favourite rhythm. Its thematic material is more rigorously developed than earlier movements in this form. The contrasting trio (G flat) sings a charming *Ländler* of the kind always heard at a sentimental *Heimatabend* in Styria.

The finale begins *pp* in B flat minor. The attentive ear will immediately pick up a significant semitone (G flat–F) in the figure for horn and clarinets, sounded against the subdued muttering of strings, and may not be wrong in drawing comparisons with the C flat–B flat relation in the first bars of the work. (It is interesting that these two semitonal relations are a fifth apart.) In both cases the semitone slips to the dominant. Tension mounts rapidly until the powerful main theme of the movement explodes at bar 43:

Ex.12

This positively defines the V–I polarity of the home key, E flat major. Again the tremendous emphasis upon the note C flat is fascinating. Almost immediately the harmony side-slips upwards a semitone from the triad G flat–B flat–D flat to the chord of D major before finally establishing E flat major after a wave-like chromatic ascent. At this point horns affirm tonic centrality with an emphatic statement of the theme of Ex. 10.

Thus far the movement has passed through a powerful enhancement of E flat tonality on the basis of the following progression:

Ex.13

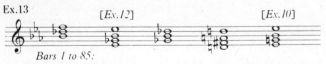

Bars 1 to 85:

Following this, the music slips away from E flat to C minor for a second thematic cluster. Such harmonic procedures give important clues to Bruckner's musical thought which Hanslick, who described the music as 'complex', totally failed to appreciate. What Bruckner does here is expand traditional step-progressions by ever-widening chromatic interpolations, exploring enharmonic relations which take the music into remote sub-regions of the central key. In earlier works, this gave him some trouble. Bruckner learned much from Wagner's technique of chromatic enhancement, whereby a passage in a given key could be enriched by temporary departures into distant tonal regions. It is also obvious that he was attracted by Schubert's enharmonic colouring. The result is not only a richly coloured and wide-ranging tonal canvas, but sometimes the discovery that harmonic exploration can overstretch lines of structural communication.

In this finale Bruckner again tries to solve the problem of unifying a great variety of thematic material in a purposive drive towards the definitive restatement of the symphony's opening theme in the home key. The momentum of exposition and development is retarded, as in the Third Symphony, by a tendency to manœuvre uneasily between thematic and harmonic options. In working with formal concepts expanding conventional sonata-form, the concept of classical sonata-form remained a subconscious obsession blocking the full flowering of his creative vision. He was to some degree hampered by latent assumptions, derived from an earlier phase of musical experience, which everyone else was only too ready to assure him were the correct ones.

Heinrich Schenker, who well understood the relation of harmonic progression to the unfolding of large-scale forms, wrote interestingly of the technique of cyclic progression:

As long as we consider as 'cyclic' only those compositions which organically join a splendid plurality of ideas . . . the underlying principle will have to be: Spare your harmonies and develop out of them as much thematic content as possible.[1]

Whereas Bruckner did indeed generate themes richly from primary harmonies, he also by no means spared his harmonies. The harmonic relations from which some of his themes grow are often adventurous and complex. Consider, for example, the main theme of the finale of Symphony No. 7. Bruckner thus made things difficult for himself as long as he thought in terms of traditional sonata-form. His harmonic procedures required something more wide-ranging than sonata-form, so that his main centres of tonal orientation are revealed as the significant moments of an integrated structure *and not as deviations from some familiar formal assumption.* If Hanslick and his followers heard Bruckner's harmonies as deviated,

[1] H. Schenker: *Harmony* (first published in 1906 as *New Musical Theories and Fantasies – by an Artist*), trans. E. M. Borgese, ed. O. Jonas (Chicago, 1954).

this was only because they were making the wrong assumptions.

Commenting on Schenker's mature views, developed long after his initial work on harmony, Oswald Jonas wrote:

A masterpiece of music is, in Schenker's conception, the fulfilment of a primary musical event which is discernible in the background. The process of composition means the foreground realization of this event. This explains the boundless wealth and power of the masters and the improvisational effects in which their works abound. The composer, his balance centred unconsciously or instinctively in the *Ursatz* [the background harmonic event] can wander unerringly, like a somnambulist, and span any distance and bridge any gap, no matter what the dimension of his work.[1]

This comment is extremely revealing when applied to Bruckner's earlier symphonies. We may wonder whether the background harmonic event was always as clear to him as it should have been. If it was not, this may have been because Bruckner's vivid harmonic imagination was at variance with familiar sonata-form assumptions. The *Ursatz* tugging at his subconscious mind could not, in fact, be squared with classical techniques of exposition, development and recapitulation. It is therefore very important for the listener to adjust his musical sensibilities to a wider arc of tonal adventure, especially when studying the great works we must now consider.

The Later Symphonies

Substantial thematic quotation must seem a *sine qua non* in discussing Bruckner's mature works, especially as an analytical volume of at least this length could easily be written about any one of them. However, thematic analysis alone is not necessarily the best approach – and in any case the days are long past when a sonata-form movement could be 'explained' by isolating the main themes of an exposition and pointing to their treatment in development and subsequent recapitulation. In Bruckner's later music, which transcends the limitations of classical sonata-form much as a waltz by Chopin transcends the dance suites of Lanner and Strauss, harmonic relationships are of the greatest interest, because it is these which decide the temporal unfolding, the tonal

---

[1] H. Schenker, *op. cit.*, editorial by O. Jonas.

organisation of large-scale sections – the *Auskomponierung*[1] of the work as a whole. We shall see, nevertheless, that for Bruckner a *theme* can also be a means of anticipating the harmonic unfolding of an entire movement. This is why Bruckner's themes often have a fascinating structure based upon the interpenetration of two dimensions, the first being the intrinsic melodic aspect of the theme itself, the second its harmonic implications. If Bruckner's melodies are not always immediately and obviously beautiful, they are always extremely interesting. It is quite certain that Bruckner did not have Mahler's melodic gift; but then he approached the formal function of melody from a different standpoint, conditioned, no doubt, by his insight into contrapuntal forms and his experience of fugal extemporisation.

The point about a fugue subject is that it contains within itself a number of structural implications: it can be inverted, augmented, diminished, worked in canon and stretto, and it can yield subsidiary figures each of which can be developed in episodic sections. Bruckner selects his themes carefully with a view to their large-scale implications for symphonic form, as he came to understand it. Therefore his themes are big with their own future, and the first sounds of a Bruckner symphony look forward to their final and wonderful end, which is always a consummation of the principle of tonic harmony. When we hear the opening arpeggio of the Seventh Symphony, we sense at once the tremendous power which is going to be generated from it; and in listening to the subsidiary thematic figures which follow the arpeggio, we divine the unfolding of the first movement. Likewise, in the Sixth Symphony, we understand the formal importance of subtle inflections in the main theme, which includes melody-notes later brought into play as secondary tonic centres when the music unfolds through regions and sub-regions of the central key. Once we understand this principle, we can see that it was, after all, foreshadowed in classical music.

Mozart's popular little pianoforte sonata in C, K545, illustrates it to perfection. In the first movement, the opening four-bar theme unfolds the simple harmonic pattern I–V–I–IV–I–V–I. Also, the second subject is derived from the first by inversion. When we study

[1] Schenker's term for the concept of 'through composition', the overall flow and progressive manifestation of a form within an archetypal structure of primary harmonies.

the whole movement, we see that its unfolding is simply an extension of the elementary progression stated in the opening tune. In a Bruckner symphony, which develops the same principle to the *n*th degree, the internal tensions generated by harmonies often distant from the main key require the structure to unfold through shifting harmonic complexes, and not necessarily according to a procession of themes outlining traditional sonata-form. Each complex is itself a large-scale sub-structure which tends to set itself against the others – until the composer finally demonstrates the unity of idea binding everything together. There is no release from the tremendous expectancy generated by such procedures until the finale ultimately explodes all tensions in tonic harmony – as in the last moments of the Eighth Symphony, which combine the main themes of the symphony in a massive contrapuntal texture. In all this, of course, there is something of Wagner, and *Tristan*, with its long-delayed resolution of the harmonic problems proposed in the opening of the music-drama, springs readily to mind as a powerful influence upon the symphonist from Ansfelden. But perhaps the fertile influences brought to bear upon Bruckner's strangely profound musical mind were equalled, if not finally transfigured, by the massive silences, the peace, beauty and spiritual richness of Upper Austria, all still very much in evidence in our own day. Undoubtedly there is a relation, even if it is difficult to define, between a composer's music and the roots from which he sprang. The responsive listener will readily detect it. Perhaps this is one of those cases where what cannot be said can only be 'shown', as Ludwig Wittgenstein, the Austrian philosopher once suggested, and not stated. Mysticism apart, Bruckner's music increasingly fascinates those who listen to it with a responsive ear.

SYMPHONY NO. 5 IN B FLAT

Classical tonality is a relationship between moving sounds with respect to a tonic centre. The determining factors in tonality are primary orientations defining this centre. Thus it is possible for Beethoven, in his First Symphony, to sound cadences in IV, VI and V before actually *sounding* C major, the key of the symphony. The three 'related keys' of C major really define the tonic focus of C before C is actually heard in explicit tonic function. In the romantic tonality of Chopin and Wagner, the concept of a system of related keys tends to dissolve in the flux of shifting harmonies. At first, there seems to be no fixed process the application of which guarantees a firm tonic. In playing a Chopin Mazurka, for example, the establishment of the tonic, after a passage during which the hands trace a rhythmic figure through veil after veil of chromaticism, seems to take place by a kind of miracle. With growing insight, we realise that even when we feel we are going to lose our way in the maze of floating harmonies, there is in fact a firm, purposive drive towards the tonic. We then understand that highly complex chromatic relationships can arise from quite simple background schemes. It is such background schemes which establish the underlying architecture of a piece.

This is what seems to happen in the Fifth Symphony, and especially in the remarkable first movement, which has an astounding introduction laying out, in the space of fifty bars, a series of massive harmonic contradictions. Yet the movement begins and ends in B flat, and the exposition of themes ends in F, the dominant. The primary harmonic form thus grows within the familiar classical formula I–V–I. However, the introduction (peculiar to this symphony), after a solemn liturgical beginning in B flat and a few moments' rest, suddenly blazes out *ff* with an arpeggiated figure in G flat major. Another rest, and a third figure is heard in A major. The arpeggio returns in B flat, and is again contradicted by the third figure, this time on the dominant of A. After one and a half bars of silence, the bass-line of the third figure is heard in diminution and inversion with new material in A major, now redirected as the dominant of D major. The themes thus exposed are shown in Ex. 14 overleaf. The last statement takes us to the *Allegro*, the note D becoming the third of the B flat chord which is, however, darkened to B flat minor with the appearance of the first subject (Ex. 15 overleaf).

Bruckner now sets out to validate this harmonic tableau, constantly avoiding B flat major by using B flat minor as a means of veering away from anything approaching conventional tonic affirmation. Thus the movement makes a wonderful journey through a series of remote keys. When the tonic arrives definitively, it sounds right because the constant chromatic fluctuation of keys has, in fact, included subtle preparations of the tonic through G minor and E flat, which have close relationships with it. Throughout the movement, which should be considered as a

Ex.14

(cf *bar 31*)

progressive unfolding of harmonic relations, the texture is enriched with a procession of fine themes treated with a wealth of contrapuntal resource, which includes massive exploration of a canon between Ex. 14(b) and Ex. 15. The entire thematic/harmonic process is a perfect demonstration of what can be done when the composer's creative instinct is centred and balanced by an underlying, if concealed, scheme of primary harmonic relations.

The *Adagio* opens in D minor with a soft pizzicato accompaniment in triplets which assume thematic importance in the scherzo. The main theme is given out first as an oboe solo, and its opening figure resembles the counterpoint of Ex. 14(c). In transition to his second theme, a passage of delicate beauty, the composer introduces a chain of falling sevenths against falling quaver triplets on the violins. The new theme has a suave majesty,

Ex.15

Allegro

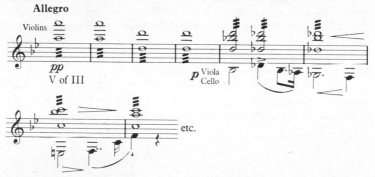

and it modulates through many keys. The rest of the movement is a contemplative unfolding of the two themes, with the falling sevenths assuming background importance. Towards the end the music sounds tenuous and austere.

The first sounds of the scherzo, also in D minor, and Bruckner's most highly organised movement in this form so far, are an accelerated version of the triplet figure accompanying the first theme of the *Adagio*. They now accompany a lean tune played on woodwind, whilst retaining and developing importance as a binding thread in the movement as a whole. They persist under a second melody introduced in slower tempo, and a third, and are heard yet again in invertible counterpoint with a sub-strain of the second theme. The first forty-six bars fall into clearly-defined harmonic sections – D minor, F, D flat, E – linked by Neapolitan and enharmonic relations leading up to the third theme. All this material is worked up at length before the trio, unexpectedly presented in 2/4 time, appears in B flat, with a tune reminiscent of the very first notes heard in the symphony. The main body of the scherzo is then recapitulated.

The finale of this remarkable work is justly celebrated on account of its unusual construction and its tremendous effect. It is completely successful. Superficially considered, it consists of an introduction derived, as in Beethoven's Ninth Symphony, from themes in the earlier movements, and then followed up with a massive fugue and a grand chorale. The fundamental difference is that the important fugue theme is introduced almost at once, and that figuration from the *Allegro* of the first movement (see Ex. 15),

47

introduced at bar 15 in the finale, contributes vigorously to the tremendous momentum set up by the fugue. The finale begins with the opening of the first movement. However, at the third and fifth bars the clarinet is heard to sound a falling octave. This is an anticipation of the fugue subject based upon it and allowed to make a partial appearance at bars 11 and 23. Following a reference to the *Adagio* and its accompanying figure (from which the scherzo is derived), the movement breaks out into a fugal exposition, *allegro moderato*, on the complete fugal theme in B flat minor:

Ex.16

(Observe the thematic connection with the figure at bar 15 which links up with the first movement.) This fugal exposition is not taken any further for the moment; instead Bruckner introduces a long secondary section in D flat based upon a new theme thematically connected with the second figure of the scherzo. This is taken to a climax, after which everything dies to a whisper with the ghost of the *Adagio*'s main theme heard against a drum-roll. There is a moment of silence . . . and then, like the last trump, the chorale theme makes its shattering appearance, *ff*, in G flat:

Ex.17

It is played on horns, trumpets, trombones and tuba. Strings respond quietly to this dramatic utterance. The chorale theme concludes exposition of the thematic material of the movement. From G flat the bass slips down a semitone to F natural. There are one and a half bars of silence after this serene reference to the dominant key of the symphony. An important harmonic point is made here: when presented in G flat, the first phrase of the chorale leads to the melody-note F, thus offering the opportunity of enharmonic change. This is what happens at bar

196; but Bruckner dwells on the Neapolitan relation F–G flat before letting everything subside in a liturgical-sounding F major.

Dr Simpson[1] is surely correct to consider all this as preludial matter. The fugue proper begins at bar 223 with the chorale as subject played on violas against a running counterpoint. It is a double fugue, whose second subject (Ex. 16) is combined with the chorale at bar 270. From here the movement develops immense energy. It is not all fugal. Fugal procedures are arrested at bar 349 as the music moves towards a tremendous climax on the basis of figures drawn from both chorale and second fugue subject. The G flat–F relation is explored again, after the climax has collapsed, for the reintroduction in F major of a secondary group previously heard in D flat (bars 67 ff.), thematically related to the second theme of the scherzo. This leads on to emphatic *fff* statements of Ex. 15 from the first movement, thrilling augmentation of the Ex. 16 fugue subject and a final tonic statement of the chorale, above that fugue subject, which carries the symphony to a wonderful conclusion.

Commentators and analysts differ on the matter of thematic unity. There are those who claim that only what can actually be heard in performance is important. This may be so; but it is a fact that repeated hearings reveal much that was previously missed. Moreover, concentration is definitely assisted by study of the score – not during, but after a performance, and just before the next. Apart from the aural experience, there can surely be no reasonable doubt that part, at least, of our appreciation of a great work of musical art is grounded in our intellectual understanding of the constructional processes involved. It can be argued that just as composition requires considerable technical skill, and therefore knowledge of the laws of sound, so the listener's role is enriched by insight into their detailed application. Whatever the truth of the matter, those interested in the thematic process, and in the complex thematic interconnections of Bruckner's thought, will find much to explore here. The symphony is a masterpiece of thematic process and harmonic architecture, demonstrating the composer's total integration of the vertical and linear functions of composition. Most of all it is a work of profound inspiration. There could be no finer demonstration of Hanslick's own view of music as 'sound in motion'.

[1] Simpson, *op. cit.*

The Sixth Symphony did not suffer the revisions and alterations to which some of the others were subjected. Here we have a shorter, more concise masterpiece, conceived by the mind which had successfully grappled with the complexities of the Fifth Symphony, in a form in which the composer left it. The symphony has a contemplative beauty, tinged not only with warm emotional colouring but also, in places, with an indescribable quality of detachment. It suggests the meditative withdrawal of a mind studying its own processes. It could almost be described as a philosopher's symphony, not on account of any association or definable content, but because the beauty of its form and the logic of its modulations reveal a mature philosophy of composition.

There is an air of authority in the sound of the opening bars. The triplets, continued well into the movement, accompany a philosophic theme stated low on the strings. Observe the chromatic alterations – G natural, B flat and F natural. They are significant clues to developments much later in the work, and are carried through into the harmonic unfolding of the first movement through the principle of the Neapolitan relationship. Thus the listener should be attentive to the technique of chromatic 'side-slipping' which inflects melodic patterns and enriches modulation. It is at the start of the recapitulation and in the coda that Bruckner reveals his special mastery. At such moments in the unfolding of a form the great composers, and notably Beethoven, often show profound insight into the relation between tonality and structure. It is the creation of expectancy combined with the element of surprise which brings the aesthetic thrill. Bruckner, approaching recapitulation, moves in a short space from E flat, through chords of G flat and A flat, to the dominant of the home key. Basses are pounding out A flat in the basic triplet rhythm when timpani enter on E natural (bar 207). The A flat changes enharmonically to G sharp and we are home. In the coda, Bruckner uses the tremendous gravitational impetus of the main theme to sweep through an immense range of modulations before homing in unerringly via a massive plagal cadence.

The beautiful themes of the *Adagio*, at times heavy with a strongly subjective emphasis, are easily identified. This movement, one of the composer's loveliest, and one of the few in which he adheres to a fairly orthodox sonata-form, establishes a concentrated intensity of feeling; but its haunting themes are only part of the story. The Neapolitan inflections of the first movement reveal their influence here in a harmonic texture unfolding a wealth of tonal relationships. The composer works with a richly-coloured kaleidoscope of sounds within a primary structure F–C–F, in other words I–V–I in F major; but this underlying harmonic shape is almost hidden behind shifting veils of harmonic sub-relationship. The first theme, with its flat sixth, is weighted with overtones of B flat minor, and the plangent oboe tune emphasises the melancholy effect (bar 5). The second subject, a lyrical contrapuntal complex, is introduced in E major and moves towards C major. Throughout the movement, Bruckner weaves a tapestry of harmonic sub-relations, and it is a musical mystery how a movement can evolve through regions and sub-regions and yet appear to be expressed in a simple framework which is hardly ever made explicit, except at the serene, contemplative end in F major. In such a case, the *Ursatz* is like a mountain shape only rarely glimpsed through moving veils of cloud illumined by a thousand rays of coloured light. The lonely wanderer on mountains and fells will know this effect, and if he is a musician he may well speculate on analogies between colour and sound.

Rhythmic and harmonic subtleties are hallmarks of the poetic scherzo, which begins in A minor. Its delicacy is brutally overshadowed by the powerful *fff* ending of the main section. The trio is remote in style from the earlier *Ländler*, and indulges in light-hearted contrapuntal interchanges between woodwind and strings. Horns have a distinctive role, and have been considered distant relations of those in Beethoven's *Eroica* Symphony.

In order to feel at home in the harmonic space of the finale, it is necessary to glance again at the opening theme of the symphony and to observe the structural force of F natural and B flat. Considered as harmonic polarities, these are again taken up in the finale, which grapples massively with their implications in a central tonality of A, announced by the opening theme:

Ex.18

Bewegt, doch nicht zu schnell

Very soon a march rhythm breaks out in A major, to be followed by this significant brass figure (bar 37):

Ex.19

(Note the V–I orientation of F–B flat in B flat minor.) After this the *Gesangsperiode*, introduced in C major, sounds serenely uncommitted. The main store of themes is rounded off with a dotted-note motive at bar 130. The development needs to be followed with special concentration, since it unfolds with great rigour. The key to much is contained in the Neapolitan relations of the symphony's opening theme.

SYMPHONY NO. 7 IN E

The key of E major is frequently associated with music of contemplation. Bruckner begins his Seventh Symphony with a warm tremolo third vibrating E–G sharp, from which emerges this wonderful theme on the cellos:

Ex.20

dim.

It is the composer's longest theme, and it opens a most beautiful work, which is deservedly loved. The vast, cathedral space within which the work evolves is given primary shape in the solemn, meditative ascent of the E major arpeggio. The first part is outlined by solo horn, the doubling emphasising the importance Bruckner placed on these first archetypal sounds. After this there are a number of subsidiary motives. The symphony is not monothematic; but a great many structural and harmonic implications are prefigured in it, as they are in the opening theme of the Sixth. The creative principle of the work is proclaimed in a musical statement of great beauty and significance. The first movement proceeds to analyse it; but there are meaningful connections with the *Adagio* and finale, both of which state themes relating to the first movement.

The organic unity of this massive work is a miracle of thematic interconnections and the rarest and most stirring sonorities, all drawn out from possibilities of harmonic enhancement hidden in an arpeggiated triad. It is rewarding to consider the opening theme from this point of view. The initial arpeggio is as plain as that in a Mannheim symphony, and it affirms the central tonality. Immediately, however, the melody begins to swing out towards the dominant, B, via A sharp and C natural (Neapolitan relation to B), and this hints at more distant regions which the harmonic unfolding of the movement is to explore. As the theme evolves the panoramic spread of modulational possibilities widens, until it returns, step by step, to the home key. The growing complexity of the melody, from its initial arpeggio to the subtle inflections of the central section, prefigures important areas of subsequent harmonic exploration.

The theme is stated twice, and the lyrical flow then continues with

Ex.21

Ruhig

p   Oboe
      Clarinet

after which there is a procession of new ideas, during which the song-like unfolding is frequently shaped by a more positive rhythmic pulse. The melodies themselves are subject to powerful harmonic undercurrents. There is always the risk of over-simplification when the mind is attracted by the force of primary harmonies; but the overall structure tends to polarise around the tonic E major and its dominant, the gravitational pull of which was strongly felt in the main theme. Ex. 21 shows also the importance of B minor. Within the elliptical progression thus generated there is a sinewy development and extension of the main ideas through a wealth of enhancing modulation. The movement ends with full restatement of the main theme; but with an important difference. Restatement begins with x in Ex. 20 in the effective subdominant A major. As Redlich points out[1] this is derived from the 'Judicare' in the *Credo* of the D minor Mass. Inherent gravitation pulls the music towards its dominant (E) which is of course the home key. When this point is reached, we hear the opening arpeggio of Ex. 20. From here to the end the music exults gloriously on tonic harmony – a wonderful, unforgettable sound which not only stirs the soul to its depths but makes the ear nostalgic for triads as the basic currency of musical experience. Nowak, in his introduction to the miniature score, emphasises the memorial aspect of this music as a tribute to Wagner, who died before its completion; but there will be many (and the writer is one) who will not dwell on Wagner whilst listening to Bruckner's Seventh Symphony.

The *Adagio*, in C sharp minor, presents a wealth of themes, all rich, noble music testifying to the force of spiritual realities in Bruckner's inner life. Only twenty days after completing the symphony at St Florian, he started work on the *Te Deum*. Whilst working on the symphony, he had revised the Masses in F minor and D minor. The solemn and meditative dignity of the *Adagio*,

[1] Redlich, *op. cit.*

combined with music of a personal nature in which the subjective
dimension is strong, combine to make it one of Bruckner's most
famous movements. The *Adagio* and the *Te Deum* share a common
ethos.

In the scherzo, Bruckner returns to his rumbustious *Ländler* vein.
The main figures of the first section are full of wild, exultant leaps
swinging through a bold range of modulations. The poetic trio
introduces an unusual two-in-the-time-of-three effect in its song-
like melody.

The finale opens with a theme related to the opening of the first
movement, and modulates to A flat. As in the first movement, there
is a prefiguring of harmonic relations which are going to be
important. Subsequently a chorale is presented in A flat, and it
should be observed that this key is the enharmonic mediant major
to the tonic. Using the chorale as pivot, Bruckner later restates it
with its tonal centre on C natural, a key already approached at the
end of the exposition. The notes E, G sharp (enharmonic A flat),
and C natural straddle the E major scale, neatly dividing it into
three major thirds. Tension is thus set up between the three
corresponding keys, and this generates the harmonic energy and
tonal structure of the movement. It is perhaps not without
significance that the interval of the major third, which is the unit of
harmonic relationship underlying this threefold antithesis, is
precisely the interval (E–G sharp) with which the symphony
began, and from which its first theme slowly unwinds. It is fitting,
therefore, that the logic of the whole scheme is crowned with
triumphant affirmation of the great ascending arpeggio of the tonic
key.

SYMPHONY NO. 8 IN C MINOR

In the last two symphonies there is a heightened subjectivity
touching springs of fervour and melancholy. Spiritual optimism
and consolation are sometimes overshadowed by the pressure of
opposing forces. Bruckner reveals something of his deeper struggles
and anxieties. The running battle with Hanslick, and with all those
who did not understand or could not respond to his music as he first
conceived it, had given the composer endless cause for depression
and concern; but there were deeper factors at work within himself.
The religious practices which moulded Bruckner's inner life, whilst

offering opportunities for withdrawal and retreat, did not stop problems of insecurity and personal relationship from pressing ever more forcibly upon him. Bruckner, in later life, mentally tired by the perplexities of his situation, was increasingly confronted by what a famous essayist called 'the purifying power of fact'. In Bruckner's case, the facts were not only the hostility of Hanslick and concern about the fate of his music; they were the facts of life and death confronted by an inherently nervous man ever more deeply aware of the realities of experience. In basic human terms, Bruckner was a deeply unfulfilled man; and though capable of great faith he had, like the rest of us, to steel himself to accept what *he* considered his private failures, and to confrontation with death. In maturity, lack of private fulfilment affected his emotional life; whereas curiosity, often of a morbid kind, about death, tinged his mind with a penumbra of anxiety. In his life, St Florian had become a haven of reassurance and world-transcending wisdom.

In the Eighth Symphony, Bruckner struggled with and sublimated his unfulfilled longings, anxieties and fears in music which seems to bind all the strands of his life experience into a musical synthesis, wonderfully symbolised in the unification of themes from all the movements of the work at the end. The Nowak score is based upon the 1890 version, in which there are a number of cuts. These were made by Bruckner, suffering under the usual pressures. When Haas edited the score, he restored the cut passages, and also included a few short fragments from the earlier version, thereby elevating musical instinct above strict musicological accuracy. The Nowak score thus deviates from the Haas score in this respect. As there is now a Nowak performing edition, we have to discriminate between the respective values of musical instinct and strict editorial discipline – with, of course, sympathetic insight into the pressures which led Bruckner to make cuts in the first place.

The symphony opens with an agitated, chromatic theme against the familiar tremolo. It has the same rhythm as the opening theme of Beethoven's Ninth Symphony. The key, officially, is C minor; but the tremolo begins on F, the dominant of B flat, before lifting at the fifth bar to G, dominant of C minor. The first phrase of the opening theme sounds clearly in B flat minor; but it drops to C at the fifth bar, thus exposing the tonic fifth – an extremely interesting move proposing a structural polarity of B flat–C minor, which dominates the movement:

Ex.22

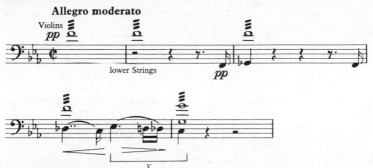

This polarity is heightened in counter-statement, and then the important falling motive

Ex.23

is immediately followed by an ascending scalic theme beginning on V of I and modulating. After a short transitional theme heard on the oboes, a third theme in E flat minor introduces a climax on Ex. 23. There is a new wave of dynamic pressure leading to a long dominant preparation of the key of E flat, in which the exposition closes with repetitions of x from Ex. 22. In the passage leading from E flat minor to the dominant of E flat there are sixteen bars of chromatic ascent. The movement in the bass is especially interesting because after this long climb the new dominant is approached from above, the result being an oblique reference in the harmonic movement to the opening theme (bars 109–25).

Development opens like a new beginning, with Ex. 22, twice augmented. Tubas hauntingly pull the harmony into E flat minor, and in a texture which is terse and incisive events move inexorably to a climax and recapitulation of Ex. 22 in B flat minor. There are two more climactic waves before the short, doleful coda, a section so dismally oppressive that Bruckner himself called it his *Totenuhr*. It conjures up an image similar to that which motivated Strauss in the first part of *Death and Transfiguration*.

After the tensions of the first movement, Bruckner places the scherzo second. It is not exactly light relief, for the two massive figures on which the first section is based are less melodies than thematic figures of tremendous energy. These figures are fully stated in the first four bars, locked in a dialectical counterpoint carrying the texture through restless key-conflict with relentless momentum. We are at a huge distance from the melodious scherzi of the earlier symphonies. In the trio Bruckner changes the tempo to a slow 2/4, and the more melodious thematic content contrasts strongly with the main section. The movement as a whole is a remarkable contribution to the history of the symphonic scherzo.

The recurring, restless chromaticism of the brooding and passionate *Adagio* is initiated early in the exposition (bar 7) with the harmonic proposition that D flat shall equal C sharp. Pressure of the flat submediant note in the opening melody darkens the main theme and colours much of the movement with an emotional stress which began with the G flat in the opening theme of the symphony (Ex. 22). The sudden transition to A major comes like a blaze of light, and the ascending arpeggio at bar 15 carries the music to a point of ecstasy. Soon a rich, roving melody is heard on cellos, followed by a solemn tuba chorale. After this eloquent and heartfelt exposition, Bruckner enters upon an extended meditation on the first theme, with canonic imitation and counter-melodies. Eventually the movement is drawn together in an ecstatic peroration and then shaded off with a contemplative coda characterised by a memory of the familiar figure from the first theme.

The opening of the finale is hectic, with wedge-shaped harmony exploding *ff* against persistent string crotchets, emphasised with *acciaccature* continuing for sixty-seven bars:

Ex.24

These stop suddenly. A new theme appears, which in turn yields to dominant preparation of E flat for a third theme heard above a repetitive rhythmic accompaniment. In the exposition of material in this movement there are frequent pauses marking off the different sections. The effect is not of hesitation, but rather of a cumulative massing of forces. Development of the main ideas is remorseless and purposive, marked by a recurring comment which has an air of prophetic solemnity:

Ex.25

Towards the end the movement swings over to a dominant pedal, above which is heard an augmented version of Ex. 22. Earlier, emphatic insistence upon its rhythm has been a factor of increasing importance. Then the horns play an augmented reference to the main scherzo figure, and this precipitates a final breakthrough to tonic major harmony.

In a triumphant C major Bruckner combines the first main theme of each movement, mastering its tensions and agonies by the discipline of counterpoint which transforms all its parts into a tapestry of exultation. He gives the basses the final C major form of the opening theme of the work, and as they stride up and down the major triad, emphasising a modified version of the figure (*x*) of Ex. 22, the rest of the orchestra is pouring out the theme of the scherzo, forced into quadruple time (upper woodwind and trumpet), the opening phrase of the *Adagio* (horns 1 and 2), and the rising sixth of the finale's main theme (*x* of Ex. 24) on trumpets 2 and 3. The binding thread is supplied by timpani which sustain a roll until the very last note, tenor and bass tubas playing the chord of C, reinforced by violas, and violins enwrapping the texture with a climbing arpeggio. In the last two bars, the whole orchestra combines in a crashing unison on the motto figure *x* of Ex. 22. This stupendous, breath-taking sound is not merely a contrapuntal *tour de force*, but rather an absolutely final dismissal of the psychological conflict hinted at in the harmonic ambiguity running through the first movement, and propounded in the C minor–B flat minor antithesis of its opening theme.

SYMPHONY NO. 9 IN D MINOR

It seems entirely natural and inevitable that Bruckner should have cast his ninth and last symphony in the key of D minor. To lovers of Bruckner's music, his Unfinished Symphony is a farewell to life, symbolised in the beautiful *Adagio*, ending in the serenity of E major with quotations from the *Adagio* of the Eighth Symphony and the opening arpeggio of the Seventh. Although Bruckner would certainly have ended in D major, it manifests in its unfinished form a kind of progressive tonality, like Mahler's Third Symphony, which also begins in D minor and (originally) ended in E major with the *Wunderhorn* song about life in heaven. However, before Bruckner's serene and contemplative ending is reached, the symphony ranges through vast and often terrifying immensities. The first two movements shed an unusual light on the *Adagio*. There can be no doubt that had Bruckner lived to complete the finale, the relationships between the movements would have been understood in their reciprocity; the musical structure of what would have surely been a massive movement would have revealed the significance of the juxtaposition of the meditative *Adagio* with the awe-inspiring depths and often fearsome visions of the first two movements. Dreams and creative visions can sometimes throw the same material into the forefront of consciousness, which then has to discipline and transcend their content. Undoubtedly the culminating glory would have conveyed the essence of this process, and reconciled the conflicts leading up to it. We can only regret that we cannot hear the final synthesis. What remains to us is a profound musical testament of heart-searching experience.

Substantial sketches for the finale were made; but they do not adequately convey an idea of the effect Bruckner ultimately intended, especially as the all-important coda is lacking. Above all, we should remember that the composer worked on this last huge conception for nine years, and had he lived longer in good health it would certainly have been extensively revised. As it was, it passed through the hands of Ferdinand Löwe, and only reached the world in a bowdlerised form in 1903. It was not heard in its original form until the performance of 1932. Despite this, Nowak, in his introduction to the miniature score, praises Löwe for his 'distinguished contribution to the memory of the master of St Florian'.

Both Bruckner and Mahler opened up immensities in their late music; the slow movement of Mahler's Tenth Symphony, with its piercing climaxes and shrieking dissonances, suggests that he too had arrived at the edge of an abyss. Mahler, however, whilst recognising the existential identity of the inner and outer worlds, had experienced no definitive illumination which convinced him that the abyss was God. One feels, in Bruckner's case, that the sublime, cathedral-like vastness opened up by the hollow D minor chord (*feierlich, misterioso*) with which the symphony begins is from the first apprehended by the composer as a *mysterium tremendum* destined to yield a culminating resolution in harmony correlative with heightened awareness.

Such vibrations resounded in Bruckner's musical soul throughout his creative life; they are his unconscious response to a 'constant' in his experience, and thus have a mantric quality beyond thought.[1] This impression would surely persist even if we knew nothing of Bruckner's religious background. That special 'quantum' of experience projected in an almost inaudible tremolo is a summons to attention. There is something peculiarly gothic about this. Centuries earlier, that very articulate and philosophical mystic, Meister Eckhart, had written of an 'essential God' beyond all reach of thought, who is yet an immanent, immediate presence in all things. The spiritual quality of Bruckner's music, often so condescendingly dismissed as a residuum of his 'simple, unquestioning faith', is far closer to the unitive, interiorised religion of an Eckhart or a Suso than it is to the merely outward forms of Catholicism. And to grasp at the sensuous beauty, or even the intellectual content, of Bruckner's music, whilst rejecting his own religious view of it, may be to reveal a peculiar insensitivity to the quality of life which has flowered in Europe in that wonderful stretch of country reaching from the Danube to the Rhine. The

---

[1] 'All that is visible clings to the invisible,
   the audible to the inaudible,
   the tangible to the intangible:
   perhaps the thinkable to the unthinkable.'   Novalis

Bruckner tremolo transmits a sensitive vibration directly to the inner ear of the mind.

It is thus that Bruckner's symphonic beginnings seem often to form in a vibrant continuum within which a vast structure is to unfold. His addiction to a symphonic device employed by Beethoven can be explained simply by saying that it justified something in *his* experience also, like a sound-image of word-transcending truth. There is also something attractive in the idea that the indefinable murmur of the life of the countryside he knew as a boy was subtly transmuted and interiorised in a symbol of the static, unchanging aspect of a mystery embracing and permeating all life and experience. In the first movement of the Ninth Symphony, Bruckner makes a final and definitive response to his own sense of the *mysterium* by grounding all action from the start in D minor. Here there are no dialectical formulae, no ambiguous harmonies. The massive opening statement, in which Dr Simpson identifies eight thematic elements, is fixed as the undeviating gravitational centre. What this might have meant in terms of a coda in the finale it is breathtaking to contemplate. The movement is best considered as a statement and counter-statement with a long coda. This view makes the most sense, and enables us to regard the recapitulation as a fusion of restatement and developmental expansion.[1] With the appearance of a theme in A major, Bruckner strikes out into an ocean of harmonic inflections; but in time he obeys the centripetal pull of D minor again before veering to F major at the end of the exposition.

At this point begins a massive restatement of all the main ideas. The opening theme is heard against itself in solemn and awesome exploration of the *mysterium*. Underlying the slow, contrapuntal unfolding is a *pp* rumble of drums and a quiet succession of minims on the strings. Timpani are carefully used to link the two main sections of the movement across the double bar. In the development of his main ideas, the composer now voyages out into wider tonal regions, and there is a heightened subjective stress. The tremendous coda swings momentously back into D minor like a planet returning on its elliptical arc. There is no release of the tension of the *mysterium*. The weight of solemn utterance is reinforced just before the concluding D minor with a strongly dissonant minor ninth, derived from bar 19 of the opening statement.

[1] R. Simpson, *op. cit.*

If there is an experiential realism about the first movement in its sombre contemplation of the unknown, the dissonant scherzo plunges into a world of nightmarish fantasy, hacking in a frenzied manner at repetitions, variants and arpeggiations of

Ex.26

Nothing is conceded to mere tunefulness, and the trio brings no relief, despite the transition to F sharp major. The whole movement is grim and tense.

The chromatic harmony with which Bruckner opens the *Adagio* is a fascinating demonstration of that free, improvisatory unfolding so characteristic of late nineteenth-century music:

Ex.27

It moves towards E, which is the gravitational centre of the movement. The loosening of tonality characteristic of this phase of

musical history is an absorbing study in the relationship between consciousness and its forms. Whereas a classical sonata-form movement always sounds like a closely-knit logical argument, a movement from a romantic symphony – subconsciously, if not always consciously, influenced by a lyrical impulse deriving from the *Lied*, an impulse which Mahler finally made totally explicit – *seems* to unfold quite freely, with many digressions and song-like episodes. The reasons for this must lie deeply in the nature of the romantic consciousness, which, in reaching out to embrace mystical immensities, entertained a view of the world quite different from that which prevailed in the eighteenth century. We like to think that eighteenth-century music reflects the spirit of rationalism and formal precision associated with the philosophy of the time. In romantic philosophy and literature there is quite clearly a preoccupation with the hidden, mysterious side of things, which suggests that the romantic principle, in all its artistic expressions, makes contact with a deeper, freely-roving dimension of the inner life hitherto inaccessible to composers, a dimension not so easily contained in symmetrical, balanced musical forms. Not without good reason could G. E. Müller, writing of Hegel's *Phenomenology of Spirit* as recently as 1959, say: 'The preface roars like a romantic symphony. . . .' Nevertheless, all Bruckner's symphonies had to move *ultimately* towards tonic major affirmation, because the innermost Bruckner had faith in the principle of a controlling centre in his own spiritual life, a faith maintained against the often desperate push and pull of his highly nervous and essentially romantic temperament. The 'dialectical ambiguity' which stalks the first movement of Symphony VIII is resolved in the final bars of the work, even though the battle is long and hard. It was impossible that his symphonies, and especially this one, dedicated *An meinen lieben Gott*, should ever end as Mahler ended *his* Ninth Symphony.

The progression of the *Adagio* is from tonal instability, through roving chromaticism, to the serenity of E major. Psychologically, the ebb and flow of the music, with its questioning repetitions of the trumpet figure:

Ex.28

etc.

mirrors the introspection of a mind which has confronted itself in its own struggles, a great musical mind whose massive achievements overcame the hell of uncertainty and self-distrust which continually plagued it.

The composer toyed with the idea of using the *Te Deum* as a finale. This might seem ideologically fitting – it certainly indicates the trend of Bruckner's mind that he could contemplate such an association between the two works; but it is not aesthetically sound. The *Te Deum* is in C major, and thus the wrong key in which to end a symphony in D minor. In any case, the *Adagio* is wholly acceptable as a final word. Its closing mood is a fitting benediction on his career.

Understanding Bruckner: a personal view

Veils of confusion were cast about Bruckner in his lifetime, and only now are they being dispersed. There was the textual problem. This was further complicated by the determination of his friends to see Bruckner as a Wagnerian symphonist. Then again, the composer always had Hanslick's antagonism to contend with. Each new symphony was the occasion for a critical diatribe, published in Vienna's leading newspaper for everyone to relish. This seemed all the more strange as Hanslick still claimed the composer as his friend, on one occasion presenting Bruckner with a signed portrait! Finally, there has been a developing tendency to build up the Roman Catholic image of Bruckner as 'God's musician', with the implication that Bruckner stands in a special relation to Catholic Christianity and cannot be enjoyed to the full unless the listener also is one of the elect. In countering this religious claim, modern criticism tries to isolate Bruckner from his religious background for the sake of getting the music into clearer perspective. Such criticism tends to make a token gesture towards the religious aspect by referring to Bruckner as a man of 'simple faith', before moving on to more interesting, and specifically musical, matters.

There can be no doubt that extra-musical associations can hinder and condition our musical appreciation, and sometimes it is very difficult to free ourselves from them. We can enjoy a sonata for flute and harpsichord without giving ideological matters a single thought. Around Bruckner, however, there is a thicket of piety which can definitely get in the way of the music.

Nevertheless, we have to see Bruckner in his totality, and it is very difficult to understand his music unless we admit the religious factor. That Bruckner did not keep his mind in watertight compartments is obvious from the Mass quotations in the symphonies, and the fact that he was often working simultaneously on both symphonies and Masses. The transference of ethos from one to the other must have been considerable; that it was so is clearly revealed in the music.

Even so, the 'simple Catholic faith' notion should be abandoned. Is there, indeed, such a thing as '*simple* faith'? After all, we do not think of composers having a 'simple' Anglican faith, or, for that matter, a 'simple' Marxist faith. *True* faith, *genuine* doubt and agnosticism all deal with immensities, and arise in the minds of those who have realised the truth of Wittgenstein's proposition: 'It is not *how* things are in the world that is mystical, but *that* it exists. . .' – together (I would add) with ourselves who observe it.

The view of Bruckner's symphonies put forward by Robert Simpson (himself a symphonist), based upon analysis of the music, requires serious consideration. Dr Simpson understands Bruckner's technique as a manifestation of 'patience', a gradual process of 'pacification' eventually leading to a blaze of "calm fire". This he contrasts with the conventional view of romantic symphonies as battlefields of desperation, struggle and stress eventually resolved by emotional release and victory over fate. The essence of Bruckner is, for him, a musical unravelling of hindrances, a 'clearing'. It is thus the finale of a work which reveals its secret, showing forth the completed form in all its beauty.

Perhaps a word could be added to this very interesting and acceptable view. The idea of 'clearing' has been somewhat popularised in recent years, and is now almost a psychological catchword used by those who feel a need to clean out the lumber of outworn attachments from their minds. There is a related interest in meditation techniques, often of Eastern origin, which encourage clearing, aiming at cool, objective assessment of experience on every level – sensuous, affective, mental and spiritual. The consideration advanced is that when all subjective complexes have been unravelled there will come a lucidity, a stability leading to the 'calm fire' of spiritual contemplation uncontaminated with

66

outworn creeds and theologies. In Buddhism, the analogy of wiping the mirror hints at the possibility of pristine vision. In Christianity, one prepares an 'upper room' to receive divine inspiration. In both cases, the clearing and sorting-out are preliminaries to a great realisation.

If there is one conviction which grows in me through increasing insight into Bruckner's creative processes, it is that the clearing technique – most wonderfully manifest in the Seventh Symphony – is a mirror to processes carried out, perhaps subconsciously, at a deep level in the composer's inner life, and that these deeper processes have indeed to do with a transcendent yet indwelling mystery. Meditation is not the sole discovery and prerogative of oriental religions. It may be deeply significant that in Bruckner's time Roman Catholic discipline encouraged laymen to withdraw into inner worlds of prayer and meditation, and allow the results of this daily practice to permeate every aspect of life. The purpose of this was to manifest a sense of spiritual priority in all things – even composing, if that was one's profession. This practice was traditional in the Christian life over many centuries and, indeed, was a vital thread in the development of western civilisation. It frequently led, as in the prayers and meditations of St Anselm,[1] to an ongoing inner dialogue, a ruminative blend of prayer and theological meditation, and it brought about both agonised self-reappraisal and moments of ecstatic vision and spiritual realisation. To ignore this in Bruckner's case is to dissociate a profound and continuous dimension of his inner life from his musical genius.

Inevitably, a life lived under such a discipline, reinforced, as in the composer's case, with frequent retreats in a great monastic foundation, would become *centred*. It would, so to speak, develop a distinctive 'tonality', would tend towards inner quietness, tranquillity, one-pointedness and spiritual intensity. The more nervous, reactive and unstable a temperament may be, the more such an ideal must appear a worthy goal. In general terms, we may suppose that the more unattainable a sense of fulfilment and spiritual rest may seem in a life plagued by self-doubt, external hostility and plain misunderstanding (as Bruckner's undoubtedly was), the more it would be idealised, together with the clearing of paths leading to it, in the processes of musical composition. And this

[1] *The Prayers and Meditations of St Anselm,* trans. Sister Benedicta Ward, SLG (Harmondsworth, 1973).

would certainly require the kind of patience Bruckner revealed in unravelling his symphonic knots.

It has been suggested that music is 'unconsummated symbol'.[1] In other words, whilst convincing us that it means something, no verbal explanation can legitimately be attempted. We have to be content with a showing forth of the musical token of experience, the abstract tonal structure on which concrete experience is, so to speak, assembled. This leaves us free, if we so wish, to find our own meaning in it, whilst affirming the aesthetic value of the musical pattern. In musical composition, experience itself, however profound its inspiration, however dynamic its innermost motivation, can recede into the background as the logical demands of tonal relationship take over. In this way, musical creation, like all art, can free the mind from self-preoccupation in the struggle to wrest form from the gross matter of life. The logic of clearing can be recognised wherever there is any selfless attempt to bring order out of chaos. It can be isolated as a key *psycho*-logical factor in all activities which begin with indeterminacy and lead patiently towards definition and organisation. Perhaps this is why Bruckner's music attracts more and more who do not accept Bruckner's religion. It may symbolise in abstract, though sensuously beautiful, terms a state of being, and a process leading to that state of being, which are instinctively felt to be a profound need of our humanity.

Yet it sometimes happens that in meditating upon the mature fruits of a dedicated mind one feels oneself to be retracing the steps of a deeply serious and meaningful journey. In Bruckner's symphonies, taken as a whole, there seems to be a stepwise progression towards sublimity of musical utterance which is reflected in individual works or even single movements. Throughout there is an inexorable momentum, a *pressure*, which eventually breaks through the inertia of one's own consciousness like a wave. Listening, for example, to the slow movement of the Seventh Symphony, I have had the conviction of something utterly real, true, overwhelmingly powerful flowing outwards from a silent, fathomless centre. It is an irresistible thought that the wonderful music in which Bruckner awakens this feeling has its origins in the purest spiritual contemplation.

[1] Susanne K. Langer, *Philosophy in a New Key* (1942).